1997 Edition of
The Exceptional Child
a way of life for mentally handicapped children

&
How To Help Your Growing Child
Through an Understanding of the Four Temperaments in Childhood

by
Ursula Grahl

ISBN 0-9524403-5-0

# The Exceptional Child
a way of life for mentally handicapped children

First Edition, 1970
Rudolf Steiner Press (ISBN 0 85440 230 6)

How To Help Your Growing Child

Through an Understanding of the Four Temperaments in Childhood

Based on the educational principals of Dr. Rudolf Steiner
First Edition – c1955 New Knowledge Books

Supplement

Euthanasia and Rudolf Steiner's Curative Education

by

Ursula Grahl

first published in
THE JOURNAL OF THE THREE ROSES Autumn, 1955 Vol. 1 No. 7

ISBN 0-9524403-5-0

© The estate of Ursula Grahl

Published by:

Anastasi ^{Ltd.}, Broome Nr. Stourbridge W.M. DY9 0HB.

All rights reserved. No part of this publication may be reproduced, stored in a retrieval system, or transmitted in any form or by any means, electronic, photocopying, recording or otherwise, without the prior permission of Anastasi Ltd.

Typeset by: ***Anastasi*** ^{Ltd.}
Printed and Bound in Great Britain by
Biddles ^{Ltd.}
Guildford and King's Lynn.
Cover by: ***Anastasi*** ^{Ltd.} Design Studio
© Cover design ***Anastasi*** ^{Ltd.} 1997

Acknowledgements

The Publishers thank Rudolf Steiner Press and Rita Stebbing New Knowledge Books for their agreement in our publishing this book, also the Society of Authors as the literary representative of the Estate of John Masefield for permission to print his poem "A Creed". We are grateful to all those friends who have helped to make the publication of this book possible.

Publishers Foreword

After many years of being out of print Ursula Grahl's well loved little book is back again, with the addition of another book of hers - "*How to Help Your Growing Child - Through an Understanding of the Four Temperaments in Childhood*" and a "*Supplement, Euthanasia and Rudolf Steiner Education*".

Due to changes in terminology over the years since the first publication of these works, between 1955 and 1970 some of Ursula Grahl's words have been altered by the editors. In trying to balance "political correctness" with the original style we have kept this to a minimum and have left in such words as ""backward", which though no longer widely used would be difficult to substitute without considerable rewriting and this we feel would depart from the original "flavour" of the text. Similarly, where "he" has been used meaning a child of either sex, this has been left unaltered. When reading this book it should also be born in mind that significant changes have been made to the rules regulating childrens homes/schools such as the government department responsible for these children has moved from health to education and the National Curriculum has been introduced since these works were written.

Contents

Publishers Foreword .... Page 3
URSULA GRAHL 1913-1980 .... Page 6

The Exceptional Child
   a way of life for mentally handicapped children .... Page 13

CHAPTER I
"I–Said the Donkey All Shaggy and Brown" .... Page 15

CHAPTER II
General Matters of Importance .... Page 24

CHAPTER III
Early Years .... Page 33

CHAPTER IV
Toys and Games .... Page 46

CHAPTER V
School Years .... Page 50

CHAPTER VI
Special Therapies .... Page 69

CHAPTER VII
Dramatic Work .... Page 71

CHAPTER VIII
The Use and Meaning of Fairy Tales… .... Page 74

CHAPTER IX
Towards Adult Life .... Page 84

CHAPTER X
The Rudolf Steiner Curative Education Movement… .... Page 88

CHAPTER XI
Reincarnation and Karma .... Page 91

CHAPTER XII
… Now Christmas Can Come .... Page 101

How To Help Your Growing Child
Through an Understanding of the
Four Temperaments in Childhood .... Page 109

Part I
THE NEED FOR SOUND KNOWLEDGE .... Page 110
THE FOUR TEMPERAMENTS .... Page 111
THE SANGUINE TEMPERAMENT .... *Page 112*
THE CHOLERIC TEMPERAMENT .... *Page 112*
THE PHLEGMATIC TEMPERAMENT .... *Page 113*
THE MELANCHOLIC TEMPERAMENT .... *Page 114*
UNDERSTANDING THE CHILD .... *Page 115*

Part II
WHY FOUR TEMPERAMENTS? .... Page 116
FINDING A BALANCE .... *Page 117*
DANGER OF THE SANGUINE TEMPERAMENT .... *Page 118*
TREATMENT OF THE CHOLERIC CHILD .... *Page 119*

Part III
TREATMENT OF THE PHLEGMATIC CHILD .... Page 121
HANDLING THE MELANCHOLIC CHILD .... *Page 122*
CONSIDER EACH CHILD INDIVIDUALLY .... *Page 124*
THE EFFECTS OF RIGHT AND WRONG HANDLING .... *Page 125*
IN CONCLUSION .... *Page 125*

Suppliment
Euthanasia and Rudolf Steiner's Curative
  Education .... Page 127

Address List
The Independent Rudolf Steiner Schools and homes for those in
  need of Special Care. .... Page 142
Bibliography: .... Page 144

URSULA GRAHL 1913-1980

Ursula Grahl was born on the 11th. September 1913 in Stadthagen near Hanover. Her father, Johannes Grahl, owned a book shop, I believe: her mother Margarete Peitmann was very artistic and interested in Anthroposopy. Ursula had a younger brother, Friedrich to whom she was most attached; and his loss at the Russian Front during World War II had a profound effect on her life.

Her childhood seems to have been idyllic and to have greatly influenced her life. She always retained a childlike wonder and enthu-

siasm in all she encountered. Ursula went to school in Berlin and was accomplished in many subjects, so that when it was time for her to choose a career she did not know what to do. She only knew what she did not want to do; that was to teach or become a nurse.

When she was nineteen years old she visited England, she went to Sunfield Children's Home, at Clent in Worcestershire, for a week-end and there she stayed for the rest of her life!

Sunfield, a Rudolf Steiner home for mentally handicapped children, the first of its kind in England, had recently opened. Here Ursula both nursed the children and taught them, the

very things she had not wanted to do. She helped in the development of a new colour therapy for the children and became the therapist.

Ursula had a great love of nature and the arts, she studied embryology, and took a special interest in astrology which she used to help her understanding of the children at Sunfield.

Above all she had a passion for fairy tales which she collected and through her study of Anthroposophy made some interpretations of their deeper meanings.

Ursula lectured regularly in Britain and Germany and wrote several books and fairy tales not all yet published.

Ursula lived and worked at Sunfield until her death in 1980 after a short illness.

Dedication

We should like to dedicate this edition to **Stanley** who is referred to in the last chapter of "The Exceptional Child". He was one of the first children to arrive at Sunfield Childrens Homes in 1931 and remained there until his death in 1997.

Publisher

The Exceptional Child
a way of life for mentally handicapped children

The Exceptional Child
Preface to the 1970 edition

This is not a textbook on work with mentally handicapped children but is a straightforward account of some aspects of the life which is lived with such children in one of the "Rudolf Steiner" Curative Education Homes in England. The work of this Home is based on the general educational principles given by Steiner in 1919 and on the special indications he subsequently gave for a number of mentally and emotionally handicapped children who were brought to him. For the further study of these principles the reader is referred to the list of books at the end of this book.

The descriptions in the following pages are all taken from real-life situations which the author has encountered in almost forty years of caring for children with afflictions of many kinds. The book is offered in the hope that this experience of working with Rudolf Steiner's ideas may be of help to the many people all over the world who find themselves having to care for a mentally handicapped child without being trained or equipped for such a task.

A final word of thanks is due to Miss Aileen Bowater for her generous help in the preparation of the manuscript and to all the friends who gave helpful comment and advice.

Ursula Grahl

CHAPTER I

"I–Said the Donkey All Shaggy and Brown"

Once again it was Christmas time. A handful of people were celebrating together the festival of the season. Though they lived in the second half of the twentieth century, they were keeping the Twelve Days of Christmas as of old.

The setting was a Home-School for handicapped children, children who from an ordinary point of view had had a poor deal in life, being afflicted in many different ways, both physically and mentally. There were children who could not walk; children who could not speak; children who were full of fear, emotionally disturbed, restless or apathetic. A few among them had been pushed from pillar to post in their early years and were already well on the way to becoming delinquent because they had been denied the security of a happy home and a sheltered childhood–the birthright of every human being–and somehow they had failed to find even one single adult to whom they could turn for love and protection. Some of these children suffered from epilepsy or diabetes; some from cerebral palsy, congenital hypothyroidism or Downs syndrome, and many others were troubled by similar kinds of afflictions. Coming from all parts of the globe, they had somehow found their way into this Home-School, and now here they were, assembled in the school hall and being helped to celebrate together the Twelve Days of Christmas.

On each of these twelve days their nurses and teachers would gather them all before the Christmas Tree to live together through the story that is told in the Gospels, the story of the Birth of the Child Jesus in the stable at Bethlehem. They would act a kind of nativity play, improvising it together, building it up from day to day, improving it and adding to it as they went along.

Some of the older children present had been in this Home-School since their infancy, and every Christmas for as long as they could remember they had experienced something of this kind. For them Christmas had become the highlight of the year, and they looked forward to it from one winter to another. But for some of them, particularly among the younger children, this was their first encounter with the story of Bethlehem and for many it was also their first experience of being accepted fully, just as they were, of being respected and recognised in their dignity, as human beings. For each child, however helpless, was to be included in the performance and be given a part to play according to his or her ability; even for the most incapable child some little task would be found that he or she could perform.

One of the teachers would tell the story, calling on the children in turn to come forward and play their parts. Another teacher would be at the piano playing the familiar old carols, or Christmas songs written by members of the staff over the years, and improvising wherever music was needed.

Leaving a large empty space in the centre of the hall to serve as the stage, people were seated in a semicircle on three sides of the room, looking towards the fourth side where there stood a tall Christmas Tree with the stable of Bethlehem in front of it.

Each day the performance would begin with the forming of a small procession to walk round the inner space. Leading this procession was one of the older girls who had been chosen to be the "Angel". Her face was radiant, for she was fully aware of her responsibility, and proudly she bore a large golden star mounted on a stick to lead the way. It was not easy for her to keep her balance while walking with slow and measured steps to the sound of one of the old carols, nor was it easy to hold the star-stick straight and keep it steady, but she did her best and improved from day to day. Wherever she went during those festive days she would joyfully announce to anyone who would listen: "I am an Angel now!" Though she would wear her apparel only during the hours of the Play–a long white gown, a pair of wings and a small crown with a golden star on her fore-

"I–Said the Donkey All Shaggy and Brown"

head–she would think of it all day long, bear herself with dignity and behave as well as any angel should.

Following her in the procession was "Old Man Joseph", a Downs boy who had never walked so straight in all his life, nor ever made such efforts to keep his mouth closed. He too was proud of his long brown garment, his hood and his staff. Behind him came "Mary", in her red dress and blue mantle, played by a little girl who had never known parents or home. She was painfully thin, dragging her feet as though she could hardly walk another step, her white little face bearing a permanent expression of sadness. The empty look in her eyes conveyed the hopelessness of her whole existence. Absentmindedly she let herself be taken along by the other children, showing not the slightest sign of pride or joy in playing the part she had been given. And yet, in the setting of this Play her manner was curiously befitting:

"Mary", who had carried her heavy burden on the long journey from Nazareth, worn out with hunger and cold, with fear and the hazards of the road, calling at the door of an inn in the hope of food, warmth and rest, but being turned away to face again the bitter wind: for there was no room at the inn! Twice the weary travellers were denied shelter and sent away with harsh words from the door of an inn. Driven to despair they dared to try their luck once more, and the third innkeeper was kind and felt sorry for them. He had no room in his house either, but he allowed Mary and Joseph to enter and rest in his stable. On the hard wooden stools, by the crib filled with straw and hay, under the dark branches of the unlighted Christmas Tree, the wayfarers settled down for the night. Beside them on the bare floor of the stable, the innkeeper had left his lantern, the only token of comfort in a hostile world.

Then gradually this hostile world was filled with wonder upon wonder: the song of the Angel, the light of the great star, the candles on the tall tree being lit as the Child was laid in the manger, the shepherds bringing their gifts and finally, during the second half of the Twelve Days of Christmas, towards the

The Exceptional Child

day of Epiphany, the Three Holy Magi appearing with their offerings of gold, myrrh and frankincense. The poor stable was filled with warmth and light, and this forlorn corner had become the centre point of the world.

A smile had appeared on "Mary's" face, there was colour in her cheeks, her movements were less abrupt and angular, something gentle had stirred in her and with lively interest she was watching now. No longer did she feel alone and forgotten, for the whole world had flocked to the stable to see the Heavenly Child, and the manger before her was filled with gifts.

While all this was taking place, another small child had been close by and he too had found, in the midst of a hitherto hostile world, his own haven of peace, a place where he was wanted, where he belonged and where he could make his home—and this was the little "Donkey" who had come with Mary and Joseph all the long way from Nazareth and who now squatted beside them in the stable in Bethlehem.

The little boy who played the part of the "Donkey" was one of those unfortunate children who are unwanted, who do not belong and have nowhere to go. Because of this he had grown ever more restless, irritable, obstinate and finally rebellious against his lot in life, until he had become maladjusted in answer to the treatment he had received from a world that rejected him. At the time of his admittance to this Home-School he had been full of mistrust and had just waited for things to go wrong again. For some time he had been quite difficult to handle, but then the unexpected occurred and he found himself included in this Play. One of the teachers had given him a shaggy coat, another had made for him a cap with two long ears, everyone had given him a friendly pat and had told him how lucky he was to be "Mother Mary's Donkey". Then he had discovered that there was even a song about him and that he was the centre of attention while everybody was singing his song:

"I–Said the Donkey All Shaggy and Brown"

*I, said the donkey, all shaggy and brown,
I carried His Mother to Bethlehem town,
I carried His Mother to Bethlehem town,
I, said the donkey, all shaggy and brown.

I, said the cow, all white and red,
I gave Him my straw to pillow His head,
I gave Him my straw to pillow His head,
I, said the cow, all white and red.

I, said the sheep with the curly horn,
I gave Him my wool to keep Him warm,
I gave Him my wool to keep Him warm,
I, said the sheep with the curly horn.

I, said the dove on the rafters high,
I lulled Him to sleep, so He would not cry,
I lulled Him to sleep, so He would not cry,
I, said the dove on the rafters high.*

Somehow all this had made a tremendous difference to the small boy, and he never looked back. For him the hour of the play had become the most important time of the day, eagerly awaited, fondly remembered and constantly talked about. Each successive day found him trotting along more happily, more full of purpose. He paid attention as never before in his life. Instead of everything going against the grain, things and events were becoming precious to him; the little boy found himself making new discoveries all the time, until in the joy and wonder of being "The Donkey" he could hardly contain himself.

Every day now he would stand by as Mary and Joseph were turned away by the first two innkeepers, but already he would be glancing ahead across the hall to where the third innkeeper was waiting with his lighted lantern, for this lantern had become to him like one of the wonders of the world, and he was looking forward to finding it placed close to him on the floor of the stable, where he would be able to watch and investigate it undisturbed while crouching by the manger of the Child.

Then there was the tall Christmas Tree, spreading its branches behind the "Donkey" and towering above him. After the lantern had been duly inspected, he would turn his attention to the tree and notice on its branches the white candles, the red roses and some strange golden shining things that were hanging down, and through the branches he would peer upward at the great gold star that was placed on the very top of the tree. Always at this early stage of the Play, when Mary and Joseph with their Donkey had only just arrived at the stable, the candles on the tree would still be unlit, and for quite a while the little "Donkey" could gaze into the mysterious dark recesses in the centre of the tree, drinking in the wonderful scent of pine needles and resin. Soon the moment would come when one of the teachers began lighting the candles on the Christmas Tree. A procession of angels would then approach the crib singing joyously, and the hall would be filled with the music of their song. From time to time the little "Donkey" would glance back over his shoulder to glimpse what was happening out there in front of the crib, but much more important for him was to watch what was happening in the depths of the tree. Somewhere among those dense branches there hung a golden crescent moon. He knew the place by now but however much he strained his eyes, he could not see it. Only when the candles came to life one after another did the crescent moon begin to shine and reflect the candlelight, so that it was suddenly there! This was a magical moment for the little "Donkey", and every day he would wait and watch for it.

Soon after the crescent moon had appeared there came another magical moment when the little "Donkey" would be called forth to worship the Child in the manger. He was the very first to come to the cradle with everyone watching him and singing his song, his very own song. Then the cow would be called, the sheep and the dove, and together they would

"I–Said the Donkey All Shaggy and Brown"

rock the cradle. After this they would all return to their various places. The little "Donkey" would slip back under the tree making sure that his golden moon was still there, and peering up through the branches at the candles and the small lit-up spaces that each created for itself.

Out in the hall many things would then be happening: shepherds sleeping in the field heard the Angel's song summoning them to the stable; the Birds' Carol would be sung and all the little children of the nursery class would be flying round as cuckoos, pigeons and doves; all the people in the hall would file past the cradle to bring their gifts to the Child; many, many things would be taking place, but the little "Donkey" would notice them only from afar. Crouching inside his tree, well hidden behind Mary and Joseph, this little boy came into his own. He had at long last found his home, a place where he belonged, where he could piece himself together and become a little person who was wanted, who was needed, who had a task to fulfil. For the first time in his life this child felt safe. The place of his heart was empty no longer, for a secret had come to dwell there, a precious secret that was golden like his crescent moon in the tree. He sat there as though in a dream. When the Play had come to an end and he was called to take off his shaggy coat and his cap with the long ears, he would nod and smile at his little moon and whisper: "Good Bye! I am coming again tomorrow!" He knew that all this wonder would not fail him but would stay there and wait for him.

Even when the Twelve Days of Christmas had come to a close–after the crowning performance of the Play on the day of Epiphany–the little "Donkey" was quite contented. He helped to put away the shaggy coat and the cap with the long ears, and did not even make a fuss when he saw the cupboard doors closing on them, for he felt assured that his treasures would be kept safe there until next Christmas, when they would be brought out again for "Mother Mary's Donkey".

The certainty of the Christmas to come shone like a guiding star through all the days, weeks and months that followed–

a distant promise coming ever nearer and filling him with joy whenever he thought of it. This golden secret which he carried always in his heart really gave him the inner stamina to face life and to begin all over again.

That Christmas time has been the turning point of the little boy's life. Henceforth he improved in his behaviour, in his health, in his ability to learn. Not, of course, that all his problems disappeared at once, but from that time his difficulties were more like those of any healthy growing child, but he had, after all, a long way to go to catch up. Previous neglect and the sad experiences of his early years had left their mark, and he was very backward for his age. But now he had good reason for wanting to take strides. With carefree joy such as he had never known before, he now set out to explore the world around him. All day long he was busily occupied, with the result that he felt a healthy tiredness in the evenings. Previously he had hated being put to bed at night, being unable to sleep and feeling lonely and afraid of the dark. Invariably he had to get out of bed and start getting into mischief, tearing his sheets and blankets, pulling down the curtains, doing everything he could in order to bring someone to his room. He did not mind if people were cross with him; all he had wanted before he came to this Home-School was to have someone there, someone to bother about him. Instead he had been given drugs to make him sleep and things had gone from bad to worse. Now there was no longer need of sleeping pills: bedtime had, in fact, become the cosiest hour of the day, when he would chat away happily about all the new conquests the day had brought him, and long before he had finished telling his story, he would fall asleep to dream of it.

It was about Easter time of the same year that a party of visitors had been conducted through the school. Among them was an elderly man who seemed very troubled at the sight of so many afflicted children. In fact, in spite of all the happy faces that greeted him everywhere, and in spite of all the evidence of positive constructive work being done to help these children, he had tentatively raised the question whether it might not be more merciful to relieve some of them of their suffering.

Now the little "Donkey" caught sight of these visitors as they were coming down a staircase, and he eyed them with curiosity. He was quick to notice the troubled expression on the face of one of them, and at once he asked:

"What is the matter with that man? Why does he look so sad?"

He paused for a moment to think. Then the reason dawned on him and he asked:

"Is that man so sad because he cannot be a donkey?"

The Exceptional Child
CHAPTER II

General Matters of Importance

When Mallory was asked, why he wanted to climb Mount Everest, his answer was: "Because it is there!"

Similarly when people ask us why we want to devote our lives to helping backward children, our answer is: "Because they are there!"

They are there indeed! They are there in far greater numbers than is commonly realised by those who do not happen to meet them, and they seem to be coming into the world at an ever-increasing rate. Though some investigators maintain that there are no more mentally handicapped children in our day than there have ever been, and that it is not the numbers that have increased but our files of information about them, there are others who state with equal authority that mental deficiency is definitely on the increase. However this may be, the fact remains that there are thousands of children in the world who need specialised care and treatment. I do not even speak of children who are classed as "educationally subnormal", but of those who are handicapped to such a degree as to be considered "ineducable". What is to be done with these thousands of handicapped children all over the world?

It is by no means easy to answer this question because opinion on the point varies considerably. Some people think that we should do all in our power to help these children; others proclaim that such children ought not to be allowed to grow up, and this view does not spring from unkindness or lack of compassion. On the contrary, it is often born out of infinite kindness and the recognition that most of these children will never become "normal", however much help they may be given and however much we may succeed in improving their condition. Even in cases where considerable progress is achieved, the patient may still be far from reaching so-called normality, far from being able to fend for himself. From the recognition of this fact

General Matters of Importance

it would appear to follow that these children are inevitably doomed to live a stunted life, a life full of misery and suffering, a life that has no purpose or goal and therefore is not worth living. To many people it seems pointless to let such a life take its course; it would be far more humane, from their point of view, to terminate it at once and thereby save a lot of suffering for all concerned.

Between these two extremes either of advocating euthanasia or being willing to spend a great deal of energy and vast sums of money in caring for such children, we find all possible shades of opinion on this vital human problem. Of course, there is an easy way out, which is to have no particular view at all on the matter. This does, in fact, apply to many people who vaguely know that this problem exists but do not make it their personal concern. They wonder why anyone should worry over something that is so far removed from most people's experience and they believe that there will still be plenty of time to begin thinking about it should necessity arise; but they hope, of course, that this necessity never will arise.

What lies behind this last argument is often the hidden fear of coming into contact with something unusual and inexplicable, something that has, moreover, the reputation of being vaguely dreadful and distressing. But running away from our fears tends, as a rule, to increase them and, above all, leaves us quite unprepared to meet them if and when they do catch up with us; and this particular problem is one that may, for no known reason, arise in the happiest and healthiest family. Thus again and again we are faced with the all too familiar situation of trying to comfort and advise distressed and bewildered parents who have suddenly found themselves responsible for a backward child in their family. It is good, in this realm, to examine our ideas before we are forced by circumstances to change them; for when a distressing situation has once arisen with the inevitable emotional strain attaching to it, it is far harder to struggle through to a clear and positive view of things. Indeed, before we can hope to offer any real help to these children or their parents, a whole jungle of wrong ideas has often to be cleared away.

There is, for instance, a very telling story of the kind lady who had been conducted round one of our Homes. At the end of her visit she said with tears in her eyes: "Poor little children! Why on earth do they all look so happy?"

The attitude of this dear lady is the attitude of many kind people the world over. Without further consideration it is for them a foregone conclusion that these children are bound, in any case, to be wretched. Now this simply is not true. On the contrary, such children are often happier and more carefree than many normal children, and life with them is never dull or empty. We do, of course, meet with some very tragic cases, but among normal human beings too we find tragic situations and the fact remains that many backward children possess great charm and have sunny dispositions.

One question is asked over and over again by visitors to our homes and schools, and this is: "Can you ever make these children normal?"

It is impossible to answer this question with a clear-cut "Yes" or "No". The situation is different in each individual case. Broadly speaking we may divide the children into four groups, and the answer will then be: firstly, there is no child, however handicapped, who is entirely unresponsive to treatment. The improvement may be very slight in relation to the enormous effort needed to achieve it, but some result, however small, will certainly emerge.

Secondly, there are many children who improve steadily over a number of years and then suddenly their illnesses begin to get the better of them and their condition gradually deteriorates. It is then much the same as with an ordinary physical illness which advances beyond the scope of medical help.

Thirdly, there are children who improve considerably, even beyond all expectation, and this improvement may be steadily maintained over a life time. Such results are encouraging indeed.

General Matters of Importance

Lastly, there are a few instances, a very few, of so-called normality being achieved, so that handicaps are overcome and the former patient is able to fend for himself and live a perfectly normal life.

Because a complete cure is comparatively rare the argument usually continues as follows: people feel that our efforts are largely wasted and wonder why we do not devote our strength, enthusiasm and experience to the education of normal children, where the work would be truly rewarding.

I do hope that this question will answer itself in the course of the following pages and that the reader will come to understand why it is that we continue in faith and confidence to help these handicapped children in their battle to conquer their afflictions.

The question: "Can you make my child normal?" is, of course, the one question that hums in the hearts of all parents who come to seek help for their children. Sometimes it is held back for fear of the verdict, sometimes it is asked right away with great anxiety, and when we have given the only possible answer—which is that we will do our very best but are unable to make any definite promise—then, often enough, the hopes of the parents seem quite shattered. For many of them it must be a complete cure for their child or nothing. Yet, in many cases, the first important step towards helping the child at all, is a clear recognition and a courageous acceptance of the truth of the situation by the parents. For many this means changing their whole attitude towards the problem. When parents stop clinging to illusions and no longer expect the impossible but have the courage to see things as they are, they will learn to appreciate even the smallest progress in their child. Like a plant that grows and blossoms in the light and warmth of the sun, so children unfold through the understanding and appreciation of those who care for them. Therefore all education of backward children inevitably begins with self-education and being flexible enough to meet them with the right attitude.

Right from the beginning we discover that subnormal children, by their very existence, are a challenge to us. We need to become inwardly mobile and must learn to break free from the accepted conviction that a child of this or that age ought to have mastered this or that chapter of learning. Nowadays even normal children are in danger of breaking down under the strain of all that is demanded of them at school.

The intellect is the undisputed king of our modern age. Before him we bow, to him we offer all we have, to him we even sacrifice our children, for intellectual cleverness is valued above all things. The reason for this is that intellectual ability is the latest achievement of this epoch in Man's history and we are justly proud of it. But the danger is that we become one-sided and omit the cultivation of other human qualities that are equally precious. Intellectual brilliance is valued so much in modern education that millions of young children suffer real misery because of the stiff examinations which hang over them from a very early age. In fact, many a normal child has, under our modern system of education, actually become maladjusted; and the obvious need is to find some way of modelling our education on the needs of the child.

If someone hopes that roses will grow in a garden where lilies have been planted and then, because they are not roses, continually destroys the lilies with the weeds as soon as they begin to grow, he will end up with a bare and barren waste instead of a garden. Yet treatment of this sort, which is obviously nonsense in relation to a garden, is applied over and over again to children, even by the parents who love them.

It is strange that when working with children we should neglect a law that is so carefully observed in every other sphere of life. Whether we are working in wood, metal or any other material we carefully look first at the qualities belonging to that material and never dream of using it for a wrong purpose. Infinitely more precious than the most valuable material in the hands of an artist is a little child in the hands of the adult who wishes to guide him on his way, help him to overcome his dangers and weaknesses, and assist him in unfolding his gifts. The child's

General Matters of Importance

difficulties may be many or few; his gifts great or very humble ones; but they are his gifts and the important thing is to encourage each child to make the most of what he has brought with him, to help him climb his own individual peak of fulfilment, and to realise that there is no uniformity in these things.

This then is a fundamental rule of all education, a rule that appears to be as difficult to apply as it is simple and obvious to understand: never try to make a child into something he cannot manage to be, but rather observe him carefully to discover what individual qualities and capacities may be slumbering in him from his birth, waiting to be called forth. Really all that is asked of a good parent or teacher is to nurse and tend these inherent qualities and help to clear away whatever hindrances and difficulties may stand in the way of their unfolding. Then in the light of understanding and encouragement they will grow of their own accord and bear fruit when the time comes. It is the birthright of every child that those responsible for his upbringing should help him to unfold the gifts he has brought with him—and there is no child, however backward, who does not bring with him some quality that is worth tending and developing. In their anxiety that the child should not be different from the accepted standards, parents can all too easily neglect or even damage the real gifts that may be there, by trying to develop skills and qualities which were never there and so could not possibly be developed. We should never attempt to eradicate what is natural to a child, in an effort to replace it by an element we may desire the child to have but which is alien to his nature. Rather should we help him to unfold and bring to freedom his inherent forces and lead them to the highest point of harmony and perfection of which they are capable in that child.

By way of example I would like to tell of a girl who was badly afflicted at birth and very backward indeed. Not only was she backward, but there seemed almost insuperable difficulties to rearing her at all. She refused her food, she bit and scratched anyone who tried to do anything for her; she kicked, screamed and got into such a state that she was almost given up as hopeless. Then at the age of eighteen months she was placed in a Home for children in need of special care. With much patience and effort it was possible over the years to clear away one hindrance after another which had impeded the child's progress. She was able eventually to attend school classes and in the end even managed to read and write, play the recorder, knit and weave, and learn many other useful occupations.

This child loved, above all, playing with water. When she was a little older and had already overcome many of her difficulties, she was allowed in the kitchen to help with washing up. Whenever she was not otherwise occupied she would turn up at the kitchen door, her sleeves rolled up, ready for the job, her eyes shining in anticipation of the enjoyment before her. With a broad smile on her face she used to knock at the door, open it slowly and peer across to the sink. If it was empty her smile disappeared. She would step right into the kitchen and begin searching round for some dirty dishes. If none could be discovered she would frown, might even get cross and stamp her foot, or she would burst into tears with the bitter accusation: "There is no washing up for me to do!" If, on the other hand, there were dishes to be washed her face would brighten and with a delighted "Ah!" she would begin tackling the job. She worked slowly and carefully, enjoying every moment of it, and it was touching to see the pink glow of satisfaction on her usually pale face when she had finished and could proudly show the results of her labours. Enormously happy at being thanked by the kitchen staff for the very real assistance she had given, she would take off her apron and say, "I'll come back again soon!", implying thereby: "And you'd better use a few implements in the meantime and provide some more work for me!"

This example illustrates one point (and there are many others) on which we might well re-examine our own views and learn to think differently about our daily work as well as about backward children. It has been drummed into us all for as long as we can remember that washing up is a bore. It is considered a dreadfully dull occupation which unfortunately has to be done over and over again. Every day we can see advertisements for better and more efficient washing up machines, because frankly people would do anything to get out of the washing up. The consequence is that the joy really has gone out of such tasks and no one enjoys doing them any longer. Yet, as we have seen, genuine satisfaction can be had even from washing up.

Someone once said to me: "You may think it queer, but I actually love sweeping; the only condition being that I must have something in front of my broom." This really means, "the more the merrier" as long as you can see some return for your labour and make a difference to the place which is obvious to everyone.

> "Who sweeps a room as for Thy laws
> Makes that and the action fine"

says George Herbert, and of course it applies equally to washing up and many other seemingly mundane occupations.

Most backward children need above all the satisfaction that comes from achievement–from work well done; and the sphere of life and work from which this satisfaction is derived matters really not at all, for we all enjoy doing the things we do well. For one person the satisfaction may come from washing up, for another from the fact that he is able to solve complex mathematical problems. Both are necessary in life and we should be grateful that different people enjoy and are good at doing different things; only, we must stop looking down on one occupation while admiring another! It really does not matter *what* a person does as long as it serves a good purpose and he enjoys doing it, and above all *does it well.*

In life much useful and necessary work has to be done which may not be particularly exciting or spectacular, but has to be done all the same. Moreover it needs to be done well. Life offers such a rich variety of occupations that it is possible to find for everyone, even the most backward child, something he enjoys and is capable of doing. It is our task to have sufficient interest and patience to study each child carefully, to get to know him thoroughly and discover, if we can, those things in him which will help him to establish himself in life and, as far as possible, find his right place in the community.

How often it happens that a backward child has his more capable class mates—or it may be his brothers and sisters—held up to him as shining examples, in the hope that he will be encouraged to follow in their footsteps; but the result, more often than not, is that he becomes discouraged, and more and more timid, until he is robbed of all self-confidence and in the end may even lose such abilities as he had already acquired.

For many people the word "education" means to fit in with a recognised standard of learning, to pass certain examinations at the right age and master a number of subjects, even though one may never need them again in later life; above all, to reach at least the average standard required to hold down the jobs that are most sought after and carry the highest salaries. But the word "education" can also mean: helping each individual child to find his own way, not to measure his achievements by the yardstick of what is generally accepted but by the light of his own personality.

The longing for fulfilment is planted deep in *every* human soul, and the stages of achievement on the road to fulfilment help man to integrate his own personality. As each individual differs from every other, the goal is by no means the same for everyone. Therefore, when setting out to "educate the ineducable" our aim should be to give each child, according to his own personal make-up, the opportunity of reaching the highest level of performance of which he is capable, leading him in fact towards the fulfilment of his own personality.

CHAPTER III

Early Years

Let us now examine the task of bringing up a mentally handicapped child from the beginning.

Again and again it happens, in the homes of rich and poor, among people of every race and country, in uncivilised parts or in highly cultured circles: suddenly people are faced with the discovery that the longed for new member of the family has been born with a deficiency which will never permit him to grow up as a "normal" human being.

Such a discovery is, of course, a tremendous shock and mostly it finds people unprepared. Such a possibility had never occurred to them, so they are bewildered and do not know what to do. Never having thought much about a problem of this kind, they have no concepts to help them understand it. When they are told that their child has Downs syndrome, congenital hypothyroidism or epilepsy, that he suffers from cerebral palsy or from phenylketonuria, they are none the wiser to begin with. Often only the vaguest ideas are associated with such technical terms, but they feel that they hide something rather dreadful, as yet unknown, the full implication of which will be brought home to them gradually, as the child grows and, with him, the problem.

People's reactions to the arrival of a handicapped child in the family are about as varied as the individuals who display them. All the same they may be roughly grouped into certain types of reaction leading to fairly predictable results. Some attitudes may be helpful, others not. If one is dealing with the parents of a handicapped child it is extremely important to start off on the right foot and avoid mistakes which will increase the burden instead of lightening it. To give exact advice on this point is very difficult. It is quite easy, of course, to do so in theory, but we must bear in mind that when people first seek help they are nearly always in a state of deep distress and probably shock. Even if they succeed in controlling their emotions outwardly, inwardly they are often engaged in a violent battle of conflicting thoughts and feelings. They are torn between hope and despair; therefore they need gentle understanding, and we must not be impatient if reason does not at once succeed in calming the troubled waters. These people must learn to adjust themselves as never before and that takes time as well as strength and goodwill.

The reaction of some parents—and the one which is of least help to anyone because it is entirely negative—is to reject the child. Unfortunately this happens more often than people realise. The reasons behind the rejection are many. It may spring from shame or pride, from guilt or fear, or from many other motives. The instinctive and spontaneous feeling of shame is still deeply rooted in people even after the good publicity the problem has received in recent years. This feeling may range from sadness and disappointment to fierce and bitter rebellion against the injustice of fate. For many parents their children are a manifestation of their own ideals and ambitions: to have a backward child is for them a lowering of their value in the eyes of the world, and a blow to their own self-esteem—this they reject. As a piece of self-knowledge it is more than they can take, so they turn away from it. Because parents are justly proud of their exceptionally bright children, it seems to them only natural that they ought to be ashamed of their backward child.

There is often, too, a feeling of guilt that is deeply rooted. The ancient question asked of Christ concerning the man who was born blind: "Master, who did sin, this man, or his parents, that he was born blind?" is still being asked today and His answer has not yet been understood. When a family faces the problem of a mentally handicapped child it is obvious that somewhere something has gone wrong, so family records are searched for possible causes. Are they to be found in the father's or the mother's family? Is the condition of the child due to certain things the mother did during the pregnancy, such as too much riding, too much driving, typing, smoking? Sometimes it is a relief to discover that the whole trouble can be put down to an accident or an illness, a severe mental strain or shock during pregnancy. Nobody then need take the blame, though of course the problem is not removed. Quite often however no obvious cause can be discovered, but a suspicion of guilt cannot be overcome, and this may drive the parents to remove the child from sight, to try and forget it, because its presence has become for them a permanent reproach and accusation.

Fear is frequently the motive for parting with the child; fear of the strangeness of the child, fear of the future, fear of what the neighbours or our colleagues may think or say, fear of our own lack of courage, skill and endurance in shouldering a task of unknown dimensions for which, to begin with, we are ill-equipped.

But whatever the motive may be, rejection of the child will not as a rule lead to any true solution of the problem. It is only shelved if we try to pretend that it does not exist—for the child does exist, and someone will have to be found to care for it. When the problem is put aside or passed on in this way the whole complex remains unresolved. Even though it may be deliberately ignored the problem tends to remain as an unpleasant shadow in the background, emerging at the slightest provocation to burden the conscience.

Strangely enough, the very same feelings of guilt that lead to rejection of a child can lead also to the opposite extreme, to what one might call "over-acceptance". This may be just as unhelpful to the child as if he were rejected. In this case the child will suffer from too much attention, too much devotion. It is just their own feelings of guilt, of having to atone for something, of needing to "make it up to the poor little thing" that can drive parents and grandparents to live henceforth entirely in the service of the child in order as they believe to make him as happy as possible. Here it is not that the parents wish to forget about the child, but they would like to make the child forget his own condition and prevent him from ever finding out that he is different from other children. This child will then be waited on hand and foot and it is a miracle if he does not become spoilt and selfish. But more serious even than this, as he will have everything done for him, never being allowed to exert himself, he will be deprived of the opportunity of learning. He will have no chance of learning even what he might have been able to learn. Increasingly as time goes on he will fall behind his own age group and in the end be far more backward and helpless than he need have been. The child may, of course, appear to be quite happy, he may thoroughly enjoy being spoilt; but as there is regress rather than progress his life is really wasted.

Such a situation may be bad enough for an only child, but it becomes worse when there are other children in the family who suffer because of it. There are cases where, in spite of the best intentions, the backward child becomes the tyrant of the family, dominating the life of the entire household, not so much because he has set himself up as a little tyrant, but because he has been made to play that part by the adults around him, who were resolved to make him the sole object of their care and devotion.

Again, it is extremely difficult to give advice in such circumstances. It is logical and humane that the afflicted member of a family should receive more care than the normal children. When money is in question, for instance, it is obvious that the handicapped child will need proper provision made for him, whereas the normal children will be capable of providing for themselves when they grow up. But it is not so much *what* is being decided that matters, but how the decision is made and whether it is reached with the understanding and willing co-operation of every member of the family.

There is a third kind of reaction which occurs quite frequently, and mostly is not really helpful either. The parents recognise with disappointment, possibly with shame or indignation, that all is not well with their child, and they determine that it must be set right before it is too late. They begin working on the child while keeping him in the background, to avoid attracting attention to him until the time comes when they hope to have succeeded in steering him into a more normal course. In their anxiety to push the child forward they may become very demanding and even hard on the child, trying to force him to perform things he cannot perform. When the child fails to achieve what is expected of him a facade is built up, a kind of superficial behaviour pattern which has been imposed on the child, and behind which the real state of affairs is concealed. The child cannot do what is asked of him; what he could learn to do is neglected as being too childish and primitive. When such children reach the age of eleven or twelve they will have become rigid and set, with an outwardly superior air, but an emptiness within. It is then very difficult if not impossible to help them to unlearn their set ways and summon sufficient inner mobility for change and progress to take place.

From feelings of shame, pride, guilt, fear, result the cases of children abandoned, children unloved and punished, children removed from sight and forgotten. For these unfortunate little ones insult is added to injury and instead of being helped and improved they tend to become worse than they need have been. Just as a tender blossom is killed by frost and enlivened by the warmth of the sun, so a parent's feelings of disappointment and resentment, contempt or indifference, are like bitter winds that freeze the tender soul of a child, whereas feelings of acceptance and understanding, as it were envelop the child in a protective atmosphere of warmth in which he can unfold and develop.

After so many discouraging examples of attitudes that are unhelpful to the child, let us look now at more helpful ways of meeting the problem and of gaining an unprejudiced approach to mentally handicapped children.

The first step should be to refrain from any kind of judgement, in particular to banish any idea of the child's inferiority. The only thing we can say with certainty to begin with is that this child is *different* from ordinary, normal children, that he is *exceptional*. This does not mean we should repress all human feelings of sadness and of true sympathy, but we should try, even in face of the initial shock of discovery, to ask the positive question: "Where do we go from here?"

We can begin by learning as much as possible about the problem that has come to meet us, endeavouring to see the arrival of such a child in the family as a responsibility and special task which life has given both to the parents and the child. Once we have decided to accept this task and to see what can be done about it, we shall no doubt turn for help and advice to those who have accepted such tasks already and have gained valuable experience in so doing.

The mother of a severely handicapped child once said to me: "I cannot tell you how grateful my husband and I are now for having had this child." (This was after years of suffering and hardship when their child had eventually won through and had become a very nice "young lady") "We owe this child a great deal for we have learnt so much from her. The difficulties she presented have led us to ask deeper questions concerning human life and destiny than ever before, and the answers we have found have given new meaning to everything. It was our child's condition which aroused these questions in us both because she made us think about things we had never considered before; we owe it entirely to her that we have come to a world-conception which now supports us and makes sense of all we have had to endure. We believe we have both become better people because of this child."

The testimony of many parents shows that although accepting a task and taking on a responsibility does not as a rule make life easier, it can make it infinitely deeper and richer. If the birth of such a child can be regarded not as a defeat but as a challenge then the battle is already half won.

In this connection we can learn a great deal from the thalidomide children. Though many of them are born without proper limbs they are as eager as normal children to participate in life and prove that it is possible to make a success of it in spite of formidable handicaps. The people who have gathered around them, determined that they should receive all the help possible, are hard at work inventing and producing aids which did not exist before. Far from being defeated by the calamity, these people have accepted the challenge and are striving to get the better of it. But it is the children themselves who are the keenest participants in this uphill battle, practising all the time with energy and courage, ready to conquer the next stage and urging their helpers to make provision for it.

Here the objection might be raised that the case of the thalidomide children cannot be compared with that of the mentally handicapped. True, the majority of thalidomide children are mentally normal, may even be exceptionally intelligent, and are therefore able to co-operate with their helpers. Co-operation is essential if progress is to be made and no improvement can be achieved without the goodwill and effort of the patients themselves. But mentally handicapped children too can be very eager to co-operate and indeed a special study is needed when a child does not wish to co-operate, but hugs his grief and will make no effort to improve. Let us, therefore, consider the difference between physical and mental disabilities; we may find that in some respects they are not as different as we imagined.

For helping the physically handicapped there is a vast field of occupational therapy. Certain movements have to be made by the patient over a certain period of time to help him regain the use of an injured limb. It is known of course that certain occupations, systematically repeated, do help to restore lost functions, also that machines can be specially designed and tools invented to exercise impaired muscles. In the same way systematic exercises can be given to stimulate and strengthen the mental faculties—exercises to improve the memory, develop presence of mind, and so on. Just as a person practises finger exercises when learning to play the violin, so there are methods of exercising the mental muscles and the following example shows how the mental faculties of a backward child can be improved so that he even begins to develop quite new capacities.

The child I am thinking of was another of those who have been more or less given up as hopeless. He was unable to learn anything because he could not concentrate on one thing for a

The Exceptional Child

few moments. He rushed about all over the place, touching everything, starting to do a dozen things but never completing anything. He had managed to pick up a few letters of the alphabet parrot fashion, and seemed to know them one moment but not the next. Occasionally he might even spell a short word correctly but a few minutes later the same word might have been quite foreign to him. The fragments of knowledge that he had picked up by chance were therefore completely unreliable. The problem was how to bring some order into this chaos and create an element of stability in the whirlpool of this child's mind. In an effort to teach him to concentrate many things were tried in vain until one day something was discovered to answer his need–this was a potter's wheel.

Something about the potter's wheel fascinated the child as nothing had ever done before and because of this he looked at it for just a fraction longer than he had ever looked at anything. To make the wheel rotate he had to move the pedal with his foot, with his hands he had to steady and form the clay, and at the same time he needed to keep his eyes on what he was doing for the clay to remain centred on the wheel. The activities of eye, hand and foot had therefore to be co-ordinated and the moment one of them failed the fact was obvious at once. Using this machine provided the boy with a means of becoming conscious of three different parts of his body, simultaneously engaged in three different activities, and by the reaction and behaviour of wheel and clay he could at every moment check and correct himself.

For that boy, learning to use a potter's wheel meant learning to concentrate. At first he could work for only a few minutes at a time, but from day to day the period lengthened until he was able to continue steadily for half an hour. His powers of concentration grew stronger and stronger while working at the wheel, but it did not remain there: he was soon able to carry this new found concentration into other activities of his daily life. From that time on the boy became in every way more calm and collected. Because at last he had the ability to attend

Early Years

to what he was doing he became gradually more skilful, both physically and mentally; order began to be established where chaos had reigned before. In this case the original purpose of the potter's wheel, to produce useful pieces of pottery, was of secondary importance, but the development of a capacity previously lacking in the boy–this was all important.

It has often been suggested that mentally handicapped patients should learn some useful craft which would enable them to contribute towards their own maintenance, and this of course is excellent when it can be achieved. But careful distinction has to be made between work for production and the use of a craft for healing purposes, such as I have just described. In the first case the quality of the object is all important; in the second the object produced matters little, but the building up of a new faculty matters above all. When we work for production we put ourselves at the disposal of the job and in the making of pottery the demands on our energy may be considerable. If a hundred cups, for example, have been thrown during the day, all will need to be turned at a certain time later. They cannot be turned while they are still wet, but must not be allowed to get too dry or they will become brittle. They must be turned at exactly the right consistency, which may be soon after throwing in very dry, warm weather, or much later in cold damp conditions. It may happen therefore that at ten o'clock at night a hundred cups, which were too wet in the afternoon, will have to be turned, as they would be too dry by morning. A task like this could never be given to a patient such as I have described. With careful training he might reach the point in later years of being able to meet such a demand, but while he is still developing faculties we need to watch him carefully to avoid strain, which would spoil everything. Therefore with every craft there is need for two departments: one for therapeutic work alone and one for production.

The example of this boy illustrates how a mental faculty can be developed through a bodily activity. In the same way many other physical activities may be adapted for developing

The Exceptional Child

different mental abilities. Occupations like knitting, weaving, woodwork, metal work, basketry, etc. are valuable not merely for the useful or beautiful objects produced but much more for the mental stimulus the patient may receive in producing them. The use of various tools in house and workshop, in garden and farm, will also have direct influence on mental capacities. Moreover the child's horizon is widened if we lead him to experience the essential qualities of the substances of the earth which are at man's disposal. It makes a great difference whether we work with wood or with clay, with sand or water, wool or metal. The individual quality and feel of these substances, their behaviour as we handle them, their hardness or softness, the tools we use in dealing with each of them—all these things can open the children's eyes to the multiplicity of the world around them.

Just as people study the special physical difficulties of thalidomide children, trying to provide corresponding aids, so we study the mental disabilities and peculiarities of afflicted children in order to discover the best treatments and exercises.

The first step then in the care and treatment of handicapped children is to get to know them well, to meet them as individuals and discover the particular problems of each child as far as possible. Then, following our observations, we look for the help we need wherever it may be found. It really means that before the child can begin to make progress we ourselves must be prepared to learn a great many new things.

We shall be guided in this process by a true knowledge of the development of the healthy child. At birth every child is a "foreigner" to the earth and must learn to adapt himself to earthly conditions. He is born with sense organs but, to begin with, he does not know how to use them; he is born with limbs but it takes time for him to walk or even grasp with his hands; he is equipped with organs of speech, but again needs time to learn to use them. Taking into account individual differences, we can, however, predict with some certainty that a normal child will reach a certain stage of development at a certain age. With a backward child this picture may alter considerably. In some achievements he may keep pace with, or even outrun the normal child; but for others he may need a much longer time, and some things he may never learn at all. It is the task of parents, nurses and teachers to help the child in the process of establishing himself in his earthly surroundings. The more deeply they understand both the child and the world in which he has to find his bearings, the better equipped they will be for the task. The natural instinct of every child is to become like the adults around him, for they have already mastered what he is only just beginning to learn; therefore he will model himself on every detail of the grown-up's behaviour. It is touching to experience the absolute trust and confidence the small child has in everyone and everything he meets, and woe betide us if this trust is betrayed. Therefore is it so important for us to be fully aware of the tremendous responsibility we bear in dealing with a little child. Though he does not yet interpret consciously what happens in his vicinity, he is none the less profoundly influenced by it. If life around him is full of confused thinking he will imitate this and his own first efforts to think will tend towards confusion. If uncontrolled emotions are let loose around him, he too as he grows up will be in danger of being governed by his own emotions. If a child is unfortunate enough to grow up in an atmosphere of lies and immorality, he will instinctively absorb these qualities too and his own character is likely to develop accordingly. When a child of eleven or twelve years is destructive or cruel, if he shows ingratitude or bad temper, it will by then be very difficult for him to change; but if the adults who care for the child when he is small are kind and considerate from the beginning, if they themselves show gratitude and are not ruled by their emotions, in most cases the child will follow of his own accord, and there will be little or no need for correction when he is older.

So we may say that all education begins with self-education. This is more easily said than done, but it really is essential for us to make as much effort in this direction as we can; and it

The Exceptional Child

will be good to establish certain habits in our own lives to help in this process. It is not for nothing that men have felt the need of prayer; but the age old custom of morning and evening prayers has been largely abandoned in our time. If we begin and end each day with just a few moments of inner concentration, thinking through the day's events and remembering where we failed, where we succeeded, and planning the morrow accordingly, this will be a source of strength and courage. We shall discover that the extra effort we make to take ourselves in hand—made on behalf of the child in our care—has direct bearing and beneficial influence in all our dealings with that child. The time spent need not be long; half an hour each morning and evening would be of great help—but it should not be forced if it means neglecting some duty. On the other hand, if we manage to spare just a few minutes here and there, we should do our best to make full use of them by giving our whole mind to helpful and positive thoughts.

In all work with afflicted children medical advice is always necessary; and many children can be helped too by a special diet. Apart from this the child's life should be organised according to common sense rules. The time table needs to be as regular as possible, particularly in regard to meals and hours of sleep. The small child should not be exposed any more than is necessary to the noise and rush of city life; a baby is a tender organism and should be allowed to develop in a sheltered place. The child can best learn to unfold the skill of his limbs and the activity of his senses in the peace of nature where sounds are gentle and things can be explored slowly and quietly. Violent experiences in early childhood could even be the cause of subsequent abnormal development even in a healthy child.

These of course are the ideal conditions, but the most necessary thing of all is that a new-born baby can be received into a happy family life, where he is loved and accepted as he is and where all members of the family—according to age, ability and time available—combine to give him what he needs. At the beginning of life the security of a happy home is all-important to every child, but particularly to the afflicted child who will need extra strength and confidence for the special battles he will have to fight and the efforts he will have to make. Unfortunately, this may be just what is lacking and it is then always difficult to find a suitable home where the child can be cared for according to his needs. But it is always the happiest solution if the early steps can be taken within the family circle to which the child belongs; there is a deep connection between parents and their children and it is of the greatest help to the progress of every child if this relationship is harmonious and happy.

The Exceptional Child
CHAPTER IV

Toys and Games

Our consideration of early childhood should not end without a few words about toys for small children. All the objects we offer a child to play with ought to be pleasant and beautiful and everything crude, ugly or distorted should be carefully avoided. The small child does not yet know the difference between good and bad, ugly and beautiful and it is a solemn thought that his own tastes in later life will almost certainly be modelled on the things we give him when he is young. Soft toys made of bright materials, wools, etc., little bells and rattles with gentle, pleasing sounds are always good. But we should definitely avoid all those hideous rubber caricatures of men and animals which often produce shrill, piercing noises into the bargain. These toys and the sounds they make may be amusing to an adult, but to the child they are meaningless and often frightening.

There is an enormous difference between what we may call a *Real* toy and the so-called toys of which, unfortunately, the shops are so full these days. It is through the activity of play that children first learn to know about the world and its activities, and their playthings will only be "toys" in the true sense of the word if they help in this process. Balls, hoops, spinning tops, pieces of wood for building, wooden toys on wheels, carts to be loaded and unloaded, houses, fences and cattle carved out of wood to make farms and villages—all such things the child will enjoy and they will also be helpful to him. By playing with toys of this kind the child is introduced in quite a natural way to the laws which operate in the world. For instance, a child who has loved ball games and has explored most of the possibilities the ball can offer, will find it comparatively easy in later years at school to understand the laws of the sphere. It is important to allow children to discover for themselves that a ball will roll easily in all directions, whereas a disc or hoop can roll in two directions only; or again to find out for themselves that although square objects can be used for building a tower, this cannot possibly be done with round ones, also that there is a limit to the height one can reach before the tower topples over, and that it makes all the difference whether his building is attempted on a bumpy, sloping surface or on level ground. It is true to say that the complicated laws and calculations which for example an architect or engineer needs to employ consciously–problems of weight, tension, carrying ability, etc.–are first explored unconsciously in the early years of childhood.

At the same time it is no good offering the small child mechanical toys, for all he can do with these is to wind them up. When he has done this a few times and knows the performance of each toy he soon becomes bored and the only thing left will be for him to take the thing to pieces and see how it works, ruining the toy and probably getting scolded into the bargain. On the other hand it is of much greater benefit to the child if we help him to construct such things as a puppet show, a windmill that really turns, or a winch that will let down a small bucket and pull it up again. Once he has done such things in play he will never forget them and it will be less difficult for him in later years to understand the principles on which they work.

One thing we have always to bear in mind when working with afflicted children; it is that they seldom have any sense of danger and are unable to guard themselves against injury in the way most normal children do. Some handicapped children are not safe to be left alone with hard objects which can be thrown, as they are liable to hurt themselves and the room they are in may be wrecked. Prevention is better than cure and it is simply asking for trouble to leave a vase of flowers on the table with the corners of the table cloth well within reach of the child who plays on the floor. Best to remove anything which might lead to trouble and give the child something that will interest him, keep him occupied and leave him no time to think of mischief. One thing which delights every child and is also extremely safe, need cost no money at all: a bag full of discarded clothes and materials of every description which he can use for dressing up will keep a child occupied for hours.

There will also be more precious toys which are brought out only when we are free to be with the child and play with him. Fragile things that need to be handled carefully, books with beautiful pictures, and so on, can then be enjoyed and the child will gradually learn by imitation to handle these as carefully as he sees the adult handling them. It is good for a child to experience both kinds of toy: the things he can have at any time, and those which can be his only under supervision and at certain special times.

We cannot leave the subject of toys without mentioning the doll, the toy which children have loved throughout the ages. The smaller the child the simpler the doll should be. When a little girl is given a perfect doll with real hair and eyelashes and all the clothes glued on she can do little else but take it to pieces and spoil it. If the doll makes a sound the mechanism inside will have to be investigated and the findings are always disappointing, if not shocking. Eyes that open and close will have to be examined too and when they break or fall out the empty sockets are a horrid sight. Much better than the elaborate and "perfect" doll will be a home made soft doll which asks to be cuddled and cannot break. It can be given a nice face embroidered or painted on and many different sets of clothes which can be taken off and on to suit imaginary occasions. But to begin with, the ideal thing for the very small child is a piece of material with five knots tied in it for head, hands and feet. When the child tires of playing with this "doll" the material can easily be tied in a different way to become a dog, a cap, a belt or a cloak. The more one can do with it, transforming it at a moment's notice into anything the occasion requires, the better. I remember once making a dolls' theatre with small children and for the dolls we used nothing but discarded neckties. Being of different materials and various colours and designs these old ties lent themselves really wonderfully to the portrayal of different characters.

The most primitive objects can often become the most use-

Toys and Games

ful toys. I once watched a little boy playing at boats in a lily pond. His "boat" was just a thick piece of wood and he was busy loading it with all kinds of objects. He had discovered that it must be loaded evenly or the boat would tilt and spill everything into the water. This was such an interesting discovery that he played for quite a long time at overloading it deliberately at one end to see how much was needed at the other to balance it again. When I returned later he had finished with this game and his boat was lying diagonally across the corner stones of the pond. I asked him what the boat was doing there out of the water and he answered: "It isn't a boat now, it's a bridge!" Some time later I saw the same beam of wood standing upright on the doorstep having been transformed into a tower.

The Exceptional Child
CHAPTER V

School Years

When the child is about three years old the need may arise for companionship of a new kind. This happens of course with every normal child. The small baby needs mainly the help and care of adults, but when he begins to move round and to speak, he looks in addition for playmates of his own age. Even in their early friendships children are already selective. According to their personal make-up they will prefer to play with one child rather than another. Later no doubt they will be grouped together according to the gifts or special interests that begin to emerge: children who are musical will meet others at the music classes, others will come together in art school or technical college, sharing their interests and speaking a common language.

In the same way the mentally handicapped child will need companionship and often this can be found in a group of similarly afflicted children. This does not, of course, preclude the possibility of friendships arising between children of different ages and with vastly differing gifts and qualities, and each may benefit greatly from such a relationship.

Now when it is suggested that mentally handicapped children are often good company for each other, there is no question of superiority or inferiority implied. Artistic people are not superior or inferior to scientifically minded people, they are merely different, nor is the handicapped child either superior or inferior, he is just *different* and this difference needs to be met in the right way. There are indeed some children who resent the company of other children and prefer to be with adults, or perhaps to be left alone altogether. But these are cases which need to be considered individually for they will require special treatment.

For many backward children of about three to four years old the ideal solution will be to go to a day centre, kindergarten or nursery school each day. There he will be able to share the life and activities of a group of children of his own age with similar needs. Moreover he will then enjoy the best of both worlds: family life each morning and evening with the secure feeling of "belonging", and during the day the stimulation and enjoyment which comes from the diversity of school life. Games and group activities are important from the social aspect and cannot be provided in quite the same way for a single child in its home. If there is no school or occupation centre near enough for him to attend daily, it might be advisable to place the child in one of the residential homes or schools for such children where he would have all the facilities of treatment and schooling he needs and where his family could visit him frequently.

I will now describe some of the essential features of life with afflicted children in a residential Home-School, in the hope that it may also be helpful to parents who are bringing up such a child at home, or caring for him in the early years until he can be admitted to one of the Home-Schools for much that is done for the children in a Home-School can also be incorporated into the life of an ordinary household and will increase the chances of development in the child.

Experience has shown that it is important for afflicted children or indeed any child living in a residential Home to preserve as much as possible the family atmosphere. They will be divided into nursery and school groups according to age and ability, though the two groups need not necessarily be the same. While it is true that all young children benefit from an orderly, regular routine in daily life, for afflicted children this is absolutely essential. It will support them in an outward frame of security and make it easier for them to gain the inner stability that is so often lacking.

It was mentioned earlier that it is good to set aside, each morning and evening, a short time of quiet for collecting our thoughts and clarifying our minds, and this applies equally to the children themselves. It really works wonders in time if we can establish a habit of beginning and ending the child's day with a prayer, a poem or a song. Many suitable prayers, verses and songs can be found and once chosen they should be repeated over long periods of time. In the evening, for instance, even when there is a regular period of playtime before going to bed or an hour of stories and nursery rhymes with the grownup, there should still be one special verse or song at the close of the day, which for the child marks the transition from waking to sleeping. This can, and should, be of deeper content, something to fill the child with confidence in the abiding truths—which means to begin with confidence in the grown-ups who are for him the bearers and representatives of these great truths. It matters not at all that such a prayer or poem may be far beyond the child's intellectual understanding. If we repeat it for him at first, later encouraging him to say it with us, he will gradually and without any special effort learn it by the daily repetition, will come to know it, and love it like a friend. What one learns in this way in early childhood is never lost but accompanies us through life and is a hidden source of strength. Though it may be forgotten for a time, some event in later life will recall it to our mind and we shall remember with conscious understanding what has unconsciously sustained us through the years.

The child will come to love this closing time of the evening if it can be treated as a small ceremony with perhaps a beautiful picture or transparency set up and a candle lighted, a time when voices are hushed and a mood of peace fills the room before the child drops off to sleep. When children are unable to sleep and are noisy after going to bed, how often it can happen that the adults call out and tell them to be quiet while they themselves continue a loud conversation in the adjoining room or have the radio or television going at full strength. But then, the louder we tell the child to be quiet the noisier he is likely to be, for the small child simply cannot help imitating all he hears and sees; and if the adult reduces his own voice to a whisper and walks through the room on tiptoe, this deliberate quietness will also be imitated by the child and it can have a truly magical effect. The best way of teaching small children is to explain as little as possible, but to do ourselves as perfectly as we can the

School Years

things we wish the child to learn. The young child learns through imitation; he will observe very shrewdly all that happens around him and will model himself on what he sees. At this stage it matters little how much the adult knows or how clever he may be intellectually. What matters above all is *what he does,* and *how* he does it. So once more we realise that self-education must come before any education of children.

In the Home-School we are describing, each day begins and closes with an assembly of all the children. The ringing of a bell, or it might be some music played or sung, is the sign for the children and their nurses and teachers to gather in the hall or school room. The various groups walk in one after another in orderly fashion and take their appointed places in a large circle. They then sing a song or speak a verse together, or both. The so-called Morning Songs and Evensongs can take many forms: a short passage from the Gospel might be read, or a verse about the day of the week, the season of the year, or a particular festival which is approaching. During these small morning and evening ceremonies it should not be necessary to tell the children what to do, but the grown-ups themselves must do as well as they can all that they wish the children to follow. If we walk in quietly, stand straight in our place with feet together and hands folded, the children will soon learn to do the same.

It may seem strange that such stress is laid on apparently unimportant things like standing straight, putting feet together and folding the hands, but there is good reason for this.

The upright position is, one could say, the hallmark of the human being. Among all the creatures that inhabit the earth, this singles man out as a creature of dignity and responsibility, one who has been "created in the Image of God". It is just here that many afflicted children are, to begin with, lacking; they find it very difficult to walk with dignity or stand upright with poise and ease. We shall, however, help the children to acquire these things much more easily if we refrain from telling them to stand straight but do so ourselves, trying at the same time to feel as strongly as possible the sense of whatever words are being spoken together at assembly. Such words might, for instance, be the following which were given by Rudolf Steiner:

Scene from the Children's Nativity Play Shepherds on their way to Bethlehem

*From my head to my feet
In the Image of God,
From my heart to my hands
His own breath do I feel,
When I speak with my mouth
I shall follow God's Will,
When I see and know God
In my father and mother,
In all loving people,
In the flowers and trees,
In the birds, beasts and stones,
Then no fear shall I feel,
Only love then will fill me
For all that is around me.*

It is the daily repetition over long periods of time, of spending just a few minutes each day to remind ourselves of the dignity of man, pausing deliberately for a while in the everyday round, to create as it were a breathing space in life, that is of such golden educational value.

So often we allow our lives to be run by the events that crop up, and consent to be pushed and hurried by demands from here, there and everywhere. How often, out of pure habit, our precious hours are spent watching the television programme which happens to be on, without even asking ourselves whether we really want to see it. It is the easiest thing in the world to slip unawares into a state where our life is spent for us, "being lived" instead of steering ourselves the way that *we* want to go. It is good to remind

The Exceptional Child

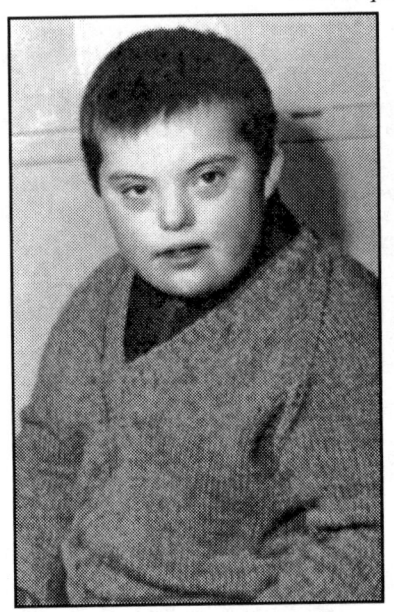

Stages of the awakening of the mind in two different children

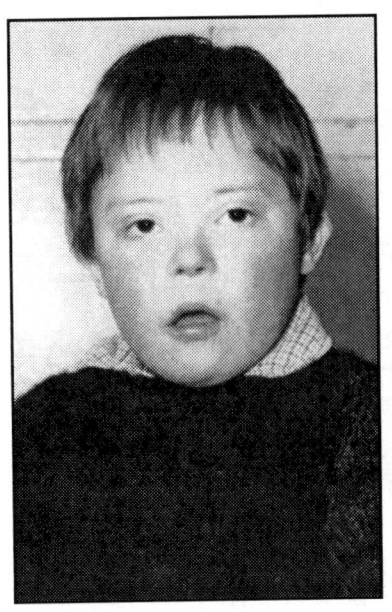

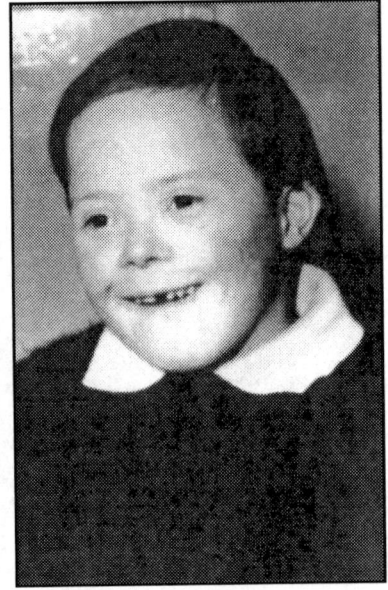

School Years

Stages of gaining confidence in two different children

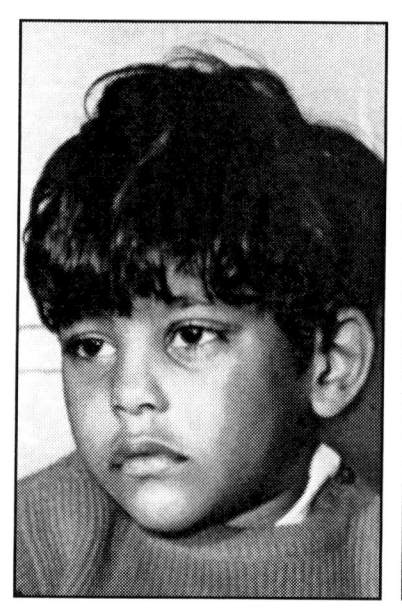

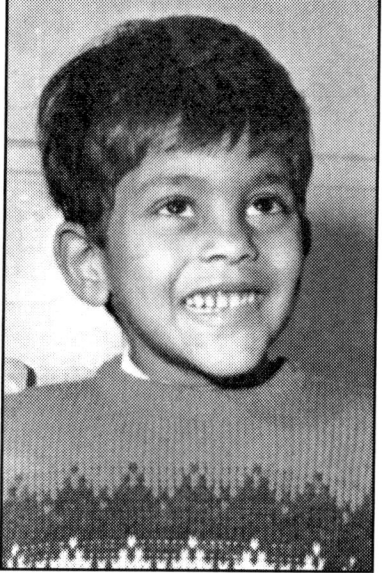

The Exceptional Child

Beginning to be creative

School Years

Scenes from a King Arthur Play

The Exceptional Child

The joy of achievement

School Years

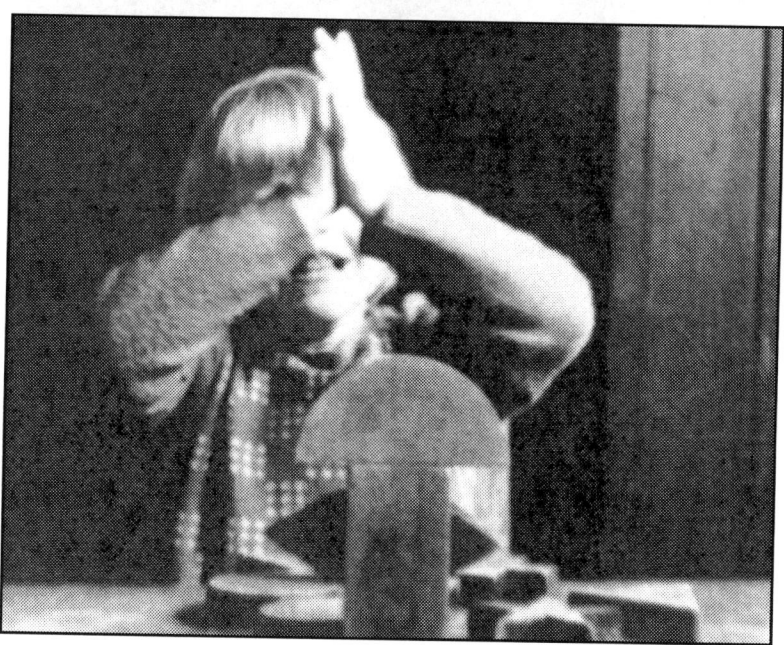

Once again it was Christmas time

ourselves from time to time of who is captain and what the goal we want to reach. Our children will benefit too if we strive for greater clarity in this way.

In our Home-School the Morning Song is followed by breakfast, and though there will always be some children who for one reason or another have to eat separately, meals are regarded as social occasions and as many as possible of the children and staff sit together and share the meal.

The same applies to all other activities of the day. The residential school should try to replace the family and home for each child, so that everything that happens concerns everyone, as it does in the family. It can often happen that, because of their peculiarities, afflicted children tend to be excluded from many activities of ordinary life; but in the Home, as part of the concerted effort towards healing and re-establishing these children, they are deliberately included in everything as far as they themselves can stand it. Just because their limitations often narrow the range of experience for such children, we should do all in our power to widen and enrich their lives.

In the Home-School I am describing Grace is spoken before every meal and all begin and finish together. Here again it is important from a pedagogical point of view to preserve as far as possible the form and style of a meal. Nowadays this can be very difficult to establish when members of a family have to come in at different times of the day. But with the afflicted child it will always pay to have meals at regular times and to treat meals as far as possible as little ceremonies. Again and again the children themselves will convey to us just how much they appreciate this and what a lot they owe to a well-ordered and happy mealtime. We see this very clearly if we watch the children at play and see them having a meal with their dolls. I remember one little girl would seat all her dolls round a table, tell them to fold their hands and then proceed to say Grace and after this a "Blessing on the meal". Before pretending to serve the meal she would say the Grace six or seven times over just because she enjoyed it so much. At the end of the meal each doll was made to say "Thank you" before leaving the table. If children have heard several forms of Grace they often repeat them all one after the other before a meal can begin and this will give the adult an idea of how much they can remember and how much they have picked up simply from daily repetition.

    The reason for building up such little formalities in the daily life is that not only do all children love taking part in small ceremonies, but that these have a strong formative power and give the children poise and confidence. Just as we like to make our rooms beautiful so too can the life lived in them be given beautiful and gracious form. Not everyone finds this kind of thing easy if they are not used to it. Take for example the adult who took part for the first time in the children's Morning Song and was obviously feeling awkward and rather embarrassed, not knowing quite what to do with his hands and feet. Next to him a normally rather clumsy handicapped child was standing perfectly at ease. Noticing the uneasiness of the visitor the child looked up at him with a puzzled expression that plainly asked "What on earth is the matter with you? Why do you have to fidget? Can't you stand still for two minutes?" In such circumstances a child may even take pity on the adult and try to put him at his ease, and it happens again and again that a backward child helps a normal adult to learn something new, something he could not easily have learnt from anyone else. The very presence of these children can lead us to do things we could not or would not do so readily without them and then we realise with gratitude that afflicted children can indeed bring great ben-

School Years

efits to so-called "normal" people—correcting, healing, opening our eyes and teaching us some common sense.

How much we owe to these children is brought home to us in many other ways. For instance when it is intended to open a new Home and School for handicapped children or provide work for handicapped adults, the right place is frequently found in the countryside, away from the noisy life of the city. Many a farmer has sold his farm and moved to an industrial area for the sake of finding easier work with shorter hours and higher wages. Certainly he may find these things as well as better shopping and entertainment facilities than in the country, but at the same time he inherits the nervous strain, the drive and restlessness that also belong to crowded cities. But these sick children, because of their needs, are often the means of taking their helpers out into the country again to a healthier life in the peace and beauty of nature. Very often relatives and friends who come from the towns or cities to visit their children remark on the great recreation they find in the setting of the Home-School and the comfort and inspiration it is to watch the activities of the children, so that they feel they have entered a new world.

A large portion of the mornings and part of the afternoons are given to lessons in the school. The time tables for the various age groups are based on the curriculum of the normal school. At the end of the book a list of publications is given so that the reader may be informed of the methods of Rudolf Steiner education which are followed in the schools I am describing. It is founded on the insight, gained through Spiritual Science, into the true nature of man and the healthy stages of childhood development. This also forms the basis for all that is done in the Rudolf Steiner Homes for mentally handicapped children, but it is understood that in each case the teacher will adapt and modify the curriculum to meet the individual needs of his handicapped children.

In Education-Therapy a subject is never introduced for its own sake or because it happens to be an accepted part of learning; but rather each subject will be examined for the help it

The Exceptional Child

may bring to the child for overcoming one of his difficulties or developing a capacity he lacks—as already described in connection with the boy who was taught concentration while working at the potter's wheel.

Naturally enough, anxious parents often enquire if their child has yet begun to read and write and learn numbers. These subjects seem to be generally accepted as the most important. Yet for an afflicted child there may be things of far greater importance for him to learn, long before he attempts reading, writing and arithmetic. Once when speaking to parents about certain moral difficulties of their child—who was in fact well on the way to becoming a juvenile delinquent—we were told:

"But these difficulties you mention, are they really so important? Since the boy is so clever, surely this will always help him to get on in life!"

Another factor also needs to be considered. The ability to read does not always turn out to be the blessing it is thought to be. Take the case of a boy who was fairly bright intellectually but who suffered from quite uncontrollable outbursts of temper. Having learnt to read he became hungry for every scrap of information he could glean, for it had dawned on him that all was not right with the world. Not satisfied with the books and papers that were given to him he would make a beeline for the daily newspapers and extract from them all the reports of accidents and crimes he could find. The effect on him was disastrous: he became very wild and began to have nightmares. Every effort was made to keep the newspapers out of his reach, but he always managed to get hold of them somehow. On one occasion when one of his friends had a birthday cake sent from home, everyone had gathered round the table to cut the cake and admire the presents, when we suddenly noticed the boy who could read busy with the box which had contained the cake. The corners had been stuffed with newspaper to protect the cake and there sat the boy reading as fast as he could all the horror stories he could find there. Another day during a walk the same boy was seen to be lingering behind and bending over some torn bits of old newspaper so brown as to render the print almost illegible; yet already he had found what he was looking for on this scrap. Afterwards he would ask endless questions, obviously trying to sort things out in his mind; but he was not really bright enough to think the problems through and come to terms with them. He would ask, for instance: "Why do people do such things when two thousand years ago Jesus Christ told us to be good? Why are we trying to be good when all the time other people are doing things they ought not to be doing?" This boy was in the Home during the war years and of course he could not help hearing about the war. His everlasting question was: "How is it possible for grown up people to be fighting one another when the message to the shepherds in Bethlehem was "Peace on earth for all men of good will?" We tried in vain to reassure this lad, to waken some other interests in him to occupy his hands and mind in a positive and helpful way; but he was too intellectual to let go of his pursuit yet not quite intelligent enough to get the better of it. In the end because of his constant state of inner conflict he became quite mad and violent. In this case it would have been a blessing indeed if he had never learnt to read.

Such examples illustrate the very real obstacles we have to reckon with all the time when working with these children and one sees how accomplishments that are valuable in the hands of one person need not be so when possessed by another.

In considering the "education" of so-called "ineducable" children, we have also to be guided by a true knowledge of the needs of normal children at a similar age. The teacher of handicapped children will therefore endeavour to give his pupils some experience of all the usual school subjects and in each he will go as far as the children are able to follow. Their ability to follow can be fostered and increased in many ways. Much can be found in Rudolf Steiner's own writings, as well as in books written by his pupils, on the art of building up a lesson. What was said in connection with the education of a normal child applies even more strongly to the education of the backward

The Exceptional Child

children. For instance to do things rhythmically is a great help and a child will be able to do in stages what he could never hope to achieve in one lesson. Rhythm saves strength and even replaces it. As every musician knows ten hours practice in a single day will not lead as far as the same number of hours spread over successive days.

CHAPTER VI

Special Therapies

The needs of many afflicted children can be fully met in a regular school life, but although classes are kept reasonably small there will always be a few in every group who need more individual attention than can be given in class. All backward children need more individual attention than healthy children and it is often not easy to group them. At first sight there may seem to be a number who need the same kind of treatment, but when we look closer we discover that what appears on the surface as a similar disability is in fact due to very different causes and therefore requires entirely different treatment.

Let us imagine we have before us several children of eight or nine years old who all suffer from the inability to communicate through speech. Now what appears outwardly as the same difficulty may be in reality the result of very different conditions: one child may be unable to speak because he was born deaf; another may be suffering from a physical defect of larynx, throat or tongue; two children may have spoken till they were between three and five years old, but then speech was lost–in the one through inflammation of the brain, in the other because of a psychological shock; a fifth child may be unable to speak because he never developed the sense for speech so the possibility of this form of communication has not even dawned on him. All these children have in common their inability to speak, but each needs entirely different treatment.

Over the years a number of special therapies have evolved out of the work such as, for instance, music therapy, play therapy, hydro therapy, colour therapy etc., and these are being developed further all the time. In this field the child himself is the main guide; for however much a therapist may have learnt from past experience which he puts to good use with all the children, he is fully aware that each new child will be different from any he has handled before. A child can open our eyes to quite new ways of helping and healing.

There are some instances where the child needs to learn a special *discipline,* which will be repeated again and again, and others where the all-important thing is that new channels of experience and communication shall be opened without imposing *any* discipline or routine. Some children will respond, at least for a time, to one kind of therapy but not to another; some children are able to benefit from them all, though at any moment the picture may change. It is therefore essential for all the people who are handling the same child to be in constant communication so that every aspect of the child's development can be co-ordinated and made available to each person concerned with him. This can only be done in an organisation where there is close co-operation between medical consultant, therapists, nurses and teachers.

From all this it will be seen that a large staff, adequate premises, and special kinds of equipment are required to meet the needs of the children. The work is therefore bound to be costly—but then it is infinitely worth while. It is not, however, the author's present purpose to elaborate the work done in the various special therapies. To do full justice to them a separate book would be needed in which each therapist could present his own account. These therapies are a matter for specialists rather than the home, and therefore they do not come within the scope of this little book.

CHAPTER VII

Dramatic Work

I would like to deal a little more fully with one important subject: the dramatic work that is done with and for the children. Some plays the children themselves are taught to act; others are performed by the adults for the children to watch. Both these are equally helpful in education.

It was already mentioned in the chapter on children's toys that all children love dressing up and acting; this is not only a pleasurable pastime however but can be of the highest pedagogical value.

Several times a year, generally for the festivals of the seasons, the teachers in the Home-School we are describing combine with their various groups of children to perform a play. Myths, legends, fairy tales, or stories from the Bible usually provide the subject for these plays. The performance can sometimes be laid on at short notice, particularly if it is a repetition of an earlier play in which several of the main actors have taken the parts before. Occasionally a play may even be improvised with a group of children who have proved themselves reliable enough, but usually the production is the work of a great many weeks. It needs careful planning, music must be written for it and afterwards learnt, and a great number of rehearsals are necessary, not only with the whole company but also with single actors and musicians. Then scenery and costumes have to be thought of and many hours spent in making these.

The play is, in the first place, not designed as an entertainment–though of course it can hardly help being entertaining when it is performed. The main object of producing it with the children is the wonderful educational opportunities it offers. It is obvious that a united effort by so many people will be a great lesson for everyone–a lesson in co-operation and learning to share. Every part will be of importance in such a play whether it is a minor character or the hero of the story, and everything depends on each person coming in at the right moment and performing his bit as well as he possibly can.

Many unforeseen things can happen during rehearsals. Sometimes children are absent and others have to step in to take their parts. When a child has enjoyed taking over such a part and has done it well he may be unwilling to give it up when the first child returns; it is not at all easy for a backward child to understand such a situation, and there are sometimes quite emotional little scenes before things get sorted out again. So during the preparation of a play there are many things to be learnt both by the children and the adults who handle them.

Choosing the children to take the various parts is also not an easy matter. A child may be given this or that part for a variety of reasons. Children who need to be reassured will probably be given parts they can act quite easily and will be given a lot of praise for doing very little. This happens, for instance, with melancholic children whose efforts will be appreciated even more than their performance warrants in order to encourage them. Some children on the other hand may be given parts that are really a little too difficult for them. Those will be the children who are already too sure of themselves and need to learn that they are not perhaps quite as superior as they think. Choleric children, for example, will benefit if they can get their teeth into a task that is just a little beyond them, and they will be using up some of their surplus energy in a good cause. When a child like this does master a quite difficult part he may not be given particular praise—everyone, apparently, taking it for granted that he can manage it.

When the play is finally performed by the children there will be many points which cannot be assessed by people in the audience who do not know the children. One child in the cast may never have acted in a play before; always having been too shy to take part in such activities he could never be persuaded to join in. But it sometimes happens that such a child comes forward quite unexpectedly during rehearsals wishing to be included of his own accord. Such a move on the part of a shy,

Dramatic Work

withdrawn child is always welcomed very warmly and he will be allowed to play the part that he fancies whether his performance is good or bad—for in this case the mere fact of his coming forward is progress indeed.

The actual performances will therefore vary greatly; in one production the whole play benefits because one child gives a particularly good performance of one of the characters; but at other times the opposite happens and the whole company has to bear with the inability or obstinacy of one child, and everyone must learn to carry this and help that child in doing so. It can also happen that a child makes a great effort to master his part, but when he succeeds he gets too sure of himself and begins to show off. Then is the time to make a change and his part may have to be given to another child whose performance will not be half as good. Even though the whole play suffers such moves have to be made for the sake of the children concerned.

Occasionally one sees a small miracle being wrought through such a play. In the excitement of the performance a child who has never spoken may call out a word, or a child who has never walked may take a step. The child himself may be shocked when he realises what he has done, but the ice has been broken and what was achieved once can be repeated. Children can become so convinced of their own inability to do certain things that they need to be taken by surprise.

CHAPTER VIII

The Use and Meaning of Fairy Tales...

As I said earlier, the subjects of plays with the children are often taken from the colourful world of mythology and folklore. People who are familiar with the education in Rudolf Steiner schools, either for normal or handicapped children, will know that the pupils, and particularly the younger ones, are encouraged to live strongly in this element of legend and fairy tale. In recent years we have heard objections to the use of fairy tales in education. People argue that it is bad for the children to live in a world of make believe, for, they say, being mere illusion it will estrange the children from the facts of real life. In curious contrast to this we find that, for example, the books of J. R. R. Tolkien have turned out to be best sellers, and people the world over seem to be hungry for just that element of wonder and magic which their modern intellect has taught them to despise as old-fashioned and primitive. In view of this it seems justified to say a few words about the real nature and meaning of legend, myth and fairy tale and the truly important part they can play in education.

Although some so-called fairy tales have sprung from the imagination of poets and writers, the authorship of the genuine old fairy tale remains obscure. These stories had been handed down by word of mouth from one generation to another until, from the time of the Brothers Grimm onward, they began to be collected and written down; otherwise they were in danger of being lost for ever.

Originally, however, the old legends and stories were not written down or invented by individuals, but were conceived in dreams at a time when the human consciousness was very different from the normal everyday consciousness of modern man. As collective dreams they appear to have sprung to life independently, and probably simultaneously, in every part of the earth, for they are archetypal pictures of the fundamental and

The Use and Meaning of Fairy Tales...

universal experiences of human life. For instance, there is hardly a country which does not possess its own version of the story of Cinderella, though each version will differ slightly—or at times considerably—from others. But in essence it is the same story and the question arises, which is the original version and which are copies with slight variations? However, these stories and legends did not in fact pass from land to land, but were directly and immediately experienced by men everywhere. It was not a question of one country adopting the tales from another but just as the sun, moon and stars, wind and weather, childhood and old age, and many other things belong to the whole of human life, so these myths and legends too were a common experience. Although fundamentally they are the same the world over, locally they may vary tremendously. The sun touches every part of the globe but the sun that shines at the polar regions appears in very different character near the equator. If you asked an Eskimo child to give a description of the sun he knows, he would probably speak with shining eyes of a faraway wonderful light that appears only rarely, kindling nature to life with its precious warmth. Because it remains for so short a time in those regions the departure of the sun is watched with deep sadness, for its absence means long months of darkness and bitter cold.

But ask an Egyptian child the same question and he will no doubt tell you of a fierce, fiery ball that is not at all far away but standing straight overhead and appearing, not at rare intervals, but on every day of the year, scorching all life with almost unbearable heat. Yet the gentle light and warmth which the Eskimo child longs for is the very same sun whose heat is dreaded at noon by the Egyptian child and from whose rays he needs to take shelter.

It is exactly the same with the archetypal facts of human life—birth and death, childhood, youth, manhood and old age—they are fundamentally one the world over, but they differ considerably if they are experienced in the South Sea Islands or in the highlands of Tibet.

The Exceptional Child

In the genuine fairy tales we have artistic, poetical presentations of such typical events in human life. The main themes are essentially the same everywhere but the details vary according to geographical locality, the epoch, and the history of the peoples. They have not been thought out in a haphazard way nor are they the products of mere fancy; but as the artist expresses his theme in music or in colour following the laws of composition, so the pictures of the genuine fairy tale are governed by definite laws. The stories are true and have deep meaning. They portray situations and problems which every human being must meet and live through at some time in his life. They do not moralise but tell quite simply and straightforwardly just what happened to someone who was like this or like that, or who found himself in this or that predicament; they show how and why he failed, or how and why he succeeded. Without sentimentality but quite objectively they picture the consequences of certain kinds of behaviour and often refrain even from judging the villain, but let him pronounce his own judgement.

Children will be able to take in the lessons of the fairy tales quite spontaneously because everything is so obvious and straightforward. They know quite well why Cinderella becomes a queen in the end and why the two wicked sisters have no hope of succeeding, for it is plain to the child that they have no one to thank but themselves. Once when rehearsing for a performance of Cinderella I overheard a group of children talking together. One of them being in a naughty mood had been annoying the others and in passing I heard another child say: "Don't be an ugly sister!" For a child to hear this from another child can often be far more effective than an admonition from an adult.

Whether a child is normal or afflicted it is the task of those responsible for his upbringing to equip him for the life that lies before him. There is no one who does not experience the whole range of human emotions at some time in his life—joy and sorrow, hope and despair, hate, love, longing, loneliness, fear, frustration, defeat or achievement. While the child listens to stories that lead him through the whole gamut of human emotions he is still safe in the care and protection of the adult who is telling the tales and he will be able slowly to build up his own faculties for dealing with these emotions later on. In this way he prepares himself for a time when he may stand alone to face them in reality. Therefore it is possible through the fairy story to give a child, in a form suitable to his age, a preparatory experience of what he must meet in adult life.

Some may think that we do not need fairy tales for this purpose but that many children's books give excellent descriptions of all that can happen in a child's day, and of the discoveries he may make living with animals on a farm, or going for a trip up the river, and so on. But there is something in each child that looks deeper, that asks for more than mere outward description of events. No doubt the child will enjoy them for a while but then he is likely to grow restless because they do not give him all he needs. Instinctively, without being able to explain what he is looking for, the child is in search of the motives and the driving force of life, these deeper powers which lie behind the outer appearance of events—and it is just these that are dealt with in the myths and fairy tales.

An example will help to make this clearer. The two pillars on which all conscious human life on earth is built are man's ability to observe and his faculty of thinking. Through all our waking hours, from morning to night, our lives are fashioned by observation and thinking. The entire structure of science rests upon these two foundation stones, for all human knowledge must be based on the capacity to observe and be expressed in clear thought.

In *observation* we must open our senses and be taken out of ourselves; *thinking* on the other hand, leads us into ourselves; it causes us to close our eyes so that we may concentrate inwardly. Man and the world in which he lives evolved together, they correspond to each other; thus the two mental activities of observation and thinking are related to the other polarities in the world around us—morning and evening, summer and winter, etc. As adults we can *discuss* these things philosophically and theoretically, but in practical life we have to *use* them, and we must teach our children to use them too.

Every child, whether normal or afflicted, must learn as he grows up to use his senses and to think. It will not help him in this if we explain the processes or discuss them philosophically; but we can help him greatly by telling him a fairy tale—in this case the story of "Snow White and Rose Red".

The two fundamental faculties of observation and thinking are pictured in the story as two sisters—children of the human soul, of every human soul. As the mother of Snow White and Rose Red lives in a little house with her two children, so the soul of every human being lives in the house of the body nurturing the two soul capacities, which need to be like sisters if the soul-life is to be healthy.

In the fairy tale, the two children say: "We will never leave each other as long as we live", and the mother adds: "What one has she must share with the other". That is exactly how it needs to be in human life: observation and thinking must never be parted and must always share whatever they have. The moment the two become separated the human being becomes unbalanced, even mentally ill. That is why we find on the one hand all the children who suffer from fixed ideas or illusions, on the other the children who are caught and imprisoned in certain limited sense perceptions that are endlessly repeated.

The story goes on to tell us that Snow White was quieter and gentler than Rose Red who liked best to run about the meadows looking for flowers or catching butterflies; but Snow White preferred to stay at home helping her mother in the house or reading to her from a big book when there was no more work to do.

These simple sentences give a true picture of the two mental activities: observation, which loves to go out and gather information; thinking, which works best at home with no outside distractions. It is thinking that keeps the house in order, and observation that brings in the treasures from without because it is ever in pursuit of lovely sense impressions—just as children catch butterflies and gather flowers in the fields.

Later we are told how the children apportion their duties. Rose Red took care of the house in summer and each morning would present her mother with a wreath of flowers; but Snow White took her place in the winter, lit the fire and polished the kettle till it shone like gold. On winter evenings when the snowflakes fell, the mother would ask Snow White to bolt the door. Yet when there came an unexpected knock she said:

"Quick, *Rose Red, open* the door!" Even in regard to such apparently unimportant things as the opening and shutting of a door the story makes no mistake, for fairy tales know what they are talking about.

It makes all the difference if the adult who tells the story has studied beforehand its deeper content and meaning. Without such understanding the telling of the story may be a pleasant entertainment, but it will remain superficial and less meaningful. Moreover, the teller should beware of making mistakes, such seemingly unimportant mistakes as, for instance, asking *Snow White* to *open* the door. When this happens the children will of course not be able to spot the mistake or comment upon it, and this is just the point: because children are not yet conditioned, as most adults are, by the modern intellectual thinking, they retain a fine instinctive feeling for what is real and true and what is not. If such mistakes are made in a story they soon begin to wonder; then they will probably ask the fatal question: "Is it really true?" Now if the adult does not know what he is dealing with in a fairy story he will probably hedge at this point and try to evade the issue. But this will only confirm the child's growing mistrust and his suspicion that all is not as it should be; he will then lose confidence in the storyteller whom he had been ready to trust completely when the story began. If, on the other hand, the adult makes the effort of finding out what a fairy tale is about, the very fact of his understanding lends weight to the story and the child is instinctively aware of this. The question "Is it really true?" will probably never be asked at all and even if it is the storyteller will be ready to meet it. He can then answer with conviction:

"Yes, it is true, every word of it; and one day when you are older you will know the truth of it for yourself"–and that is true also, for the day will come when in maturity the child will be able to understand the faculties of the human soul, and among them the vital part that is played by observation and thinking, those two pillars which support all human knowledge.

To the children themselves the adult will, of course, not explain the inner meaning of the fairy story. He will tell it quite simply, but the whole manner of the telling will say to the child: "You had better listen carefully because this concerns you. It is not the story of someone else who has nothing to do with you or who may not even exist. This whole story is speaking of you yourself and the things you do from morning to night. The mother in the story is your own soul, and just as this mother brings up her two daughters carefully, so all the time you are bringing up your own faculties of observation and thinking."

The beginning of the story of Snow White and Rose Red deals mainly with these two important faculties of man, but later other things are brought in and also there are of course many more fairy tales which deal with the countless other facets of human life; other faculties besides observation and thinking have to be developed in childhood and great problems and obstacles can be encountered on the way. There are many bridges to be crossed while the human being is living through the different stages of development from the taking of a child's first step, to the speaking of its first word, the change of teeth, the onset of puberty, right up to the final coming of age with the twenty-first birthday. It is quite astonishing to realise that there is not a single aspect of human life which is not spoken of in some fairy tale, always in very simple pictures with no sentimentality but just telling what happened and how one person failed and another succeeded. If we think about it we shall realise that children need different stories at different times of their lives, and the children themselves will be our best guides in selecting the most appropriate tale to tell. If we have chosen wisely the children will ask for the same story again and again until they have received from it all they need. When we tell stories in this way we shall find that the children are all ears; they listen as though they had never heard anything so wonderful before and urge us to repeat it again and again; but now, we must be very careful to tell each story in exactly the same way each time. Fairy stories must never be lightly changed, for the fundamental truths of which they speak do not change; and the children themselves really need to have it strongly confirmed day by day that the great truths of life stand firm. All genuine fairy stories tell the truth and from this point of view it is sad that people frequently use the phrase "Don't tell fairy tales" to mean that someone is really telling lies and they can't believe a word of it. Yet it is only lack of understanding which has led to the fairy tale being discredited in this way.

We have only attempted to interpret the first two pages of the story of Snow White and Rose Red, but we could of course have continued consistently through the whole story, and not only this one, for such deeper meanings are to be found in all genuine fairy tales, myths and legends. Rudolf Steiner spoke of these things and threw new light on that wonderful heritage of mankind, the folklore that has come down to us from olden times. The myths are very similar to fairy tales only they belong to a different sphere. Whereas the fairy tale deals more intimately with the development of the single human soul, the myths present us with wider pictures which embrace the evolution of nations, peoples, tribes and races. Every race of people has its own story of the creation of the world for example and a comparative study of these is infinitely revealing and worth while. After all, the Bible itself begins and ends with some of the grandest mythological pictures.

Folklore, of course, belongs to the earliest times, long before the appearance of the modern intellect, when people still, as it were, "dreamt" the truths of the world and of the universe instead of grasping them in the form of scientific concepts. This does not mean, however, that the lessons of the old folklore are no longer valid; the truths of the world never change but only man's way of interpreting and understanding them. Nor will the scientific concepts of the present day be the last form of knowledge; other stages of science will surely follow and our present approach be reckoned old fashioned. People have a curious way of looking down upon earlier forms of knowledge as though they automatically lost their validity with the appearance of later forms. We tend to forget that the earlier forms of knowledge have been the stepping stones which led to our present stage of development, and indeed that we could never have arrived at this stage if the ground had not been firm under our feet. When we grow up we apparently leave behind the successive stages of development belonging to the years of childhood, but this does not mean that the way a child looks at the world is wrong. It is right and necessary for him to meet the world as he does and the adult cannot attain his maturity of judgement without first passing through the phases of childhood. It is a wonderful fact that every growing child repeats, in the course of only a few years, all the stages of consciousness that have evolved in man through the ages, from the earliest epochs of his history. The child finally "catches up" as it were and reaches the level that is normal for present day man. It is this that makes childhood eternally charming: that we are allowed to travel again the path we travelled long ago. Because, as adults, we become rooted and set in the trends of our own time, as though they could never change but would remain for all eternity, it is truly refreshing to listen to a child, to look for a moment through his eyes and see how the drab, grey world of ordinary things takes on magical beauty as of old. That is why fairy tales and children belong together: the stories of "Once upon a time" were born long ago out of that dream world in which the small child still lives until he wakes up in maturity to the consciousness of our present time.

Many backward children, however, never leave this dream

world because they never manage to reach the level of our age—this, in fact, is often just what makes a child "backward", that he retains in adult life a form of mind which belongs to an earlier epoch. It does not, of course, apply to every exceptional child, but it does to many of them; it is possible, however, for the opposite condition to occur. There are some children who anticipate in an abnormal way certain features of the mind which belong to the future. Naturally they are unable to cope with these or have control over them because they have not yet been evolved in the right way at the right time. The child is, as it were, overtaken by these abnormal faculties and is at their mercy for a while—at the same time being, of course, quite out of step with the normal people and conditions of today. When such children improve and become more normal they lose these faculties which were making them ill.

Although as we said children and fairy tales belong together, it does not mean that these stories are exclusively for children or that they have nothing to offer an adult. As adults of the twentieth century we need to discover again the ancient truths of the world; but when we seek to grasp them in the forms of current philosophy or through the intellectual interpretations of our time, they very easily remain merely theoretical. Many people have had to battle with such a book as Rudolf Steiner's *Occult Science* because they found it so difficult to link the great truths that are given there to the realities of present day life. But when we find the corresponding truths presented to us in the fairy tales in very simple, homely pictures, yet telling us of those same lofty and apparently far-removed conditions that belonged to earlier stages of our planetary evolution, our grey intellectual concepts are suffused with warmth; they become a reality to us because these imaginative pictures are so full of life.

The Exceptional Child
CHAPTER IX

Towards Adult Life

When backward children have got beyond school age they will begin training in one or more of the practical occupations with which they have already become acquainted in school. Older boys and girls often develop considerable skill in many kinds of crafts; but most of all they love to take their place beside the adults in the day-to-day work which needs to be done. Their great longing is to be able to do what they have always seen the grown-ups doing, for this confirms for them their dignity as capable and valuable human beings. They love learning to work with tools, to be allowed to use a polishing machine or a washing up machine, and for them *work* is *pleasure* because it gives them grown up status. They think nothing is more wonderful than to stand beside the adult and share responsibility for the job on hand.

Experience shows that it is possible to go a long way with training of this kind and again we will take a particular child as an example, though many similar stories could be told. The child in question was a typical Downs syndrome: charming, affectionate, full of fun—and very full of mischief. He loved water—moving, rushing water—and it was quite impossible for him to pass a tap without turning it on as far as it would go. Given the slightest chance he would slip off to the bathroom, put plugs into baths and basins and turn all the taps full on. Almost beside himself with excitement he would watch and listen to the water, until someone below noticed water beginning to pour through the ceiling and rushed upstairs to find the cause. With this child scolding or punishment achieved nothing—in fact he was so delighted at the commotion he had created that one could almost feel a sneaking sympathy with him. It really seemed to be worth it every time! No matter what precautions were taken he managed again and again, with lightning speed, to lay on some drama: even when safety taps were installed in all baths and basins he discovered an ingenious way of tampering with them. Worse than water taps, however, were the gas taps. These had to be fixed out of reach and boxed in, which made things very awkward for the staff when they were in a hurry. When the boy reached school age and had to walk from one building to another for his lessons, he could not be trusted to go alone. The distance was short but there were too many temptations on the way. So he was never allowed out of sight and during walks had to be held firmly by the hand. No amount of talking did any good; the moment he saw his chance all else was forgotten, and it seemed as though he was literally compelled to precipitate some disaster, come what may.

However, very slowly over the years this child did gain control of his emotions and by the time he was approaching twenty he could be trained to lay tables in the dining room and could even be trusted to work with taps in the pantry. He also used bowls and buckets of water for washing tables, worked at the sink or washing up machine and there was no longer any fear that things would get out of hand. More important still, the boy eventually reached the point where he could safely be allowed to light the gas taps in the food-heater. He knew what time this had to be done and no supervision was necessary. He was cheerfully occupied from morning to night, working harder and harder and taking on one duty after another, until he had accumulated such a time table of jobs that for the sake of his health it was insisted that he take a day off each week. He was thrilled to be having "days off" like the rest of the grown up staff and found plenty of things to do in his free time, but he was so fond of his dining room and pantry work, and felt so deeply responsible as a member of the staff, that he could not resist looking in even on his free day, just to make sure that all was in order and nothing had been forgotten. If people showed surprise at seeing him on his holiday he would explain, almost apologetically, that he wanted to make sure everything was all right. The ridiculous thing was that quite often on these days things were not all right because the perfectly capable adult who was relieving him did the job only once a week and was unused to the routine. Before anyone realised that anything was wrong the boy would quietly step in and come to the rescue.

Such accounts could be multiplied, and curious discoveries have sometimes been made when one of these older patients was taken ill. If a member of staff fell ill provision had to be made for his work to be covered, but when one of the "children" went to bed there was usually no need for this. However, on some occasions people were continually discovering that this, that or the other job had not been done, and on investigation found it was because one of the older "children" had been kept in bed. By evening everyone had begun to realise, with a certain amount of astonishment, just how much work some of these young people had quietly taken on–simply because they loved to work and had nothing they liked doing better. The jobs had not been given to them, but they saw things which needed to be done and had taken responsibility for them.

To this encouraging account it should be added that though many patients do develop a real sense of responsibility as they grow up, they would still be unable to fend for themselves in the world or take on an ordinary paid job. In their actual work they may need no help at all and can be of great assistance to others, but most of them still need the presence around them of the people they know and who know them. For the sake of keeping them on an "even keel" and to ensure stability and continuity, someone should be near to see that all goes well. This does not mean holding their hands, they may in fact resent too much supervision, but it helps them to hear an appreciative word from time to time, to receive an encouraging smile in passing, or perhaps be cheered up with a little joke; above all there is always someone there whom they can call on in case of need. If people pass them by and are not interested, can't be bothered to get to know them or, worst of all, if they think them peculiar and look down on them, then the old troubles which had appeared to be quite overcome may show themselves again very quickly. Older patients are often extremely sensitive; they can feel a person's attitude even when nothing is said. Everyone who has worked with mentally handicapped people knows that his own inner attitude towards them is of even greater importance than all one does outwardly by way of teaching. Whether the subject is reading, writing, weaving, sewing, digging or pushing a wheelbarrow, if the teacher is himself at all impatient, if he is restless, or above all if he feels any contempt for the inability of his pupil–if there is the slightest idea in his mind that the mentally handicapped person is at all inferior to the so-called normal person–then all his teaching skill will avail him nothing. The patient will simply lose confidence, even "go to pieces", and will reject his teaching. Again it is brought home to us that he who wishes to teach others must first put his own house in order. True, people who have helped patients through many years of difficulties and know them well can safely employ a little teasing to jog them out of a groove, but very often the mere presence of an understanding person–doing nothing in particular–will smooth things out and prevent trouble arising.

CHAPTER X

The Rudolf Steiner Curative Education Movement...

The Curative Education Movement which is connected with the name of Rudolf Steiner began at a time when very little was being done for afflicted children even in civilised countries.

In answer to a request by teachers of normal children to help them with their teaching problems, Rudolf Steiner had already brought forward quite new principles of education on which the first Rudolf Steiner Schools—or Waldorf Schools—were founded. These educational principles were based on Rudolf Steiner's deep knowledge of the Being of Man and the laws that govern the unfolding of the human physical and mental faculties during the years of childhood and adolescence. Realising the far-reaching possibilities of this new approach to education, three people then asked Rudolf Steiner if it would be possible to start something similar for the afflicted child. This was the beginning, and Rudolf Steiner then gave a course of twelve lectures on Curative Education. Unfortunately he was unable to go further for he died very shortly after this course had been given.

Twelve lectures on such a vast subject may seem very little indeed to work on, but all who have studied them find they are an inexhaustible source of inspiration. Rudolf Steiner deals here with the fundamental aspects of man's nature in such a way that the contents of the lectures seem to grow greater the more we work with them; through them we can gain ever deeper insight into the riddles of human destiny.

Over the years more and more people have joined the Curative Education Movement and the work has become known in almost every part of the world. Parents' Associations have been formed which are enormously helpful because they make it possible for parents of handicapped children to meet and compare notes. It still happens all too often that the parents of such children find themselves isolated by their problem, and it helps greatly for them to meet others in a similar situation with whom they share a common experience and to speak of their difficulties with those who really understand.

In the realm of Education-Therapy too there has been a gradual process of integration and co-ordination of ways and means; all over the world people are hard at work to find out and establish still more ways of helping the children and of overcoming the problems they present. Much has already been achieved in this field, but the range is so vast and there are so many possibilities still to be explored that we must continue to look to the future for the full unfolding of Education-Therapy.

A Creed

I hold that when a person dies
His soul returns again to earth
Arrayed in some new flesh-disguise;
Another mother gives him birth;
With sturdier limbs and brighter brain
The old soul takes the road again.

Such is my own belief and trust;
This hand, this hand that holds the pen,
Has many a hundred times been dust,
And turned as dust to dust again.
These eyes of mine have blinked and shone
In Thebes, in Troy and Babylon.

All that I rightly think or do,
Or make, or spoil, or bless or blast,
Is curse or blessing justly due
For sloth or effort in the past.
My life's a statement of the sum
Of vice indulged, or overcome.

The Exceptional Child

I know that in my lives to be
My sorry heart will ache and burn
And worship unavailingly
The woman whom I used to spurn,
And shake to see another have
The love I spurned, the love she gave.

And I shall know, in angry words,
In gibes and mocks, and many a tear,
A carrion flock of homing birds,
The gibes and scorns I uttered here.
The brave word that I failed to speak
Will brand me dastard on the cheek.

And as I wander on the roads
I shall be helped, and healed and blessed;
Kind words shall cheer and be as goads
To urge to heights before unguessed.
My road shall be the road I made,
All that I gave shall be repaid.

So shall I fight, so shall I tread,
In this long war beneath the stars;
So shall a glory wreathe my head,
So shall I faint and show the scars,
Until this case, this clogging mould,
Is smithied all to kingly gold.

JOHN MASEFIELD

CHAPTER XI

Reincarnation and Karma

During this century more and more people have come to realise the truth of reincarnation. The late poet laureate, John Masefield, whose poem "A Creed" preceded this chapter, is only one of many who have expressed their deep conviction that our birth is not an absolute beginning, that the human soul does not come into existence for the first time with the creation of the body, but rather that the soul puts on this body like a garment to be worn for a time until it is discarded at death. We have long been familiar with the famous lines by Wordsworth:

> *Our birth is but a sleep and a forgetting:*
> *The Soul that rises with us, our life's star,*
> *Hath had elsewhere its setting,*
> *And cometh from afar.*

This knowledge of reincarnation and karma is not new; when we look for it we shall find it throughout history. It has gone through many different stages and has found different forms of expression in religion and philosophy. It is a truth which, above all others, can make a profound difference to our whole outlook on life, and particularly so in the realm of work with children who are born with an affliction.

Although Masefield's poem states this truth, that each human individuality passes through many different lives on earth, so clearly and plausibly, many people no doubt say with a smile:

"Ah, but that is only the poet's imagination—a poetic vision: it should not be taken as truth." But those who say this should remember how often the so-called vision of a poet, the prophetic words of a seer, have been proved true in the light of subsequent events—truer even than the reports which later record the bare facts.

Among all who in recent centuries have spoken about man's

repeated lives on earth, Rudolf Steiner was the one who felt it essential for this ancient knowledge to be brought strictly into line with modern scientific thinking in order that men could receive it and understand it again, for he knew that it must once more enter not only into religion, but into every sphere of man's life.

Before taking the subject further I would like to answer one objection which comes up again and again: many people have difficulty in accepting the idea of repeated lives on earth because they believe it is not to be found in the Bible, particularly not in the New Testament, so they feel it cannot be part of the Christian teaching. But again if only we look for it we shall find it, even in the New Testament.

I have already referred briefly to the story of the man who was born blind which is told in Chapter Nine of the Gospel of St. John. "And as Jesus passed by, he saw a man which was blind from his birth. And his disciples asked him, saying, Master, who did sin, this man, or his parents, that he was born blind? Jesus answered, Neither hath this man sinned, nor his parents: but that the works of God should be made manifest in him."

This story very clearly refers to the fact of reincarnation, for if the soul of man arose only from his present, material body, and if his individuality came into existence for the first time only with the birth of this body, no man could have existed before his birth and there would then be no sense in asking the question "Has *he* sinned?" any more than there would be in the answer Jesus gave: "No, *he* has not sinned, nor his parents…" – for remember this man had been blind from birth. True, the parents might have sinned before their child was born, but the child himself could not possibly have sinned before he even existed. Only if the child had existed before birth could such a question be asked.

We cannot dismiss such a passage in the New Testament lightly, supposing it to be just a figure of speech, or that Jesus and His disciples were unaware of the implications of what they were saying. Each word of the Gospel has been weighed and

Reincarnation and Karma

tested and is charged with deep meaning.

As well as making it very clear that the fact of reincarnation was well known to Jesus and His disciples, there is another important thing which this story would bring home to us. We are told: "Neither hath this man sinned, nor his parents: *but that the works of God should be made manifest in him*". It appears that Jesus was using the encounter with this man who was born blind as an opportunity to open the eyes of His disciples to the riddles of human destiny, which can be summed up in the word Karma. In particular Jesus was drawing attention to a great change which was then taking place regarding the laws that govern human destiny. It was as if Jesus wished His disciples to ask the question, which made it possible for Him to give the answer—an answer they needed in order to understand the great things that were happening.

In reading the Gospels we can notice again and again how situations are, as it were, created in order to make people ponder and to arouse questions in them; for where there are no questions there can be no answers. So often it happens in life that vital information we could have gained passes us by because we have not begun to look out for it, or because we are not yet ready to receive it. Even when we are seeking an answer to some question, it may in fact already have been given to us but we fail to recognise it as the answer we want. Only later when we are more mature do we at last understand and realise that the true answer to our question was close to us all the time but that we were too blind to see it.

We know that the birth of Christ was the turning point in the history of mankind. It was a new beginning to which Christ sought to open the eyes of those who were willing to see, and to teach them that the laws which had been valid for thousands of years were now to be completely transformed through His coming. This, in fact, is what the Gospel story of the man who was born blind seeks to convey to us: the realisation that the times were changing and that one ancient law in particular was now to be altered and must give place to the new law of Christ.

The Exceptional Child

Throughout the ages of pre-Christian times men's lives had been governed by the stern law of "an eye for an eye and a tooth for a tooth". In ancient times people still knew, through their old, atavistic powers of clairvoyance, that a person who was afflicted at birth had generally inherited his condition through the sins of his parents, or in consequence of his own sins committed in some previous life on earth: hence the question "Has he sinned?"

Nowadays for the majority of people the old clairvoyance has disappeared to make way for our modern consciousness which takes account of the purely material aspects of the world and works with the more immediate connections between physical cause and effect. Even so, the instinctive feeling of shame or guilt which is still felt by many parents whose children are in any way handicapped from birth, is in fact nothing else than a last lingering remnant of the insight of former times: that afflictions were to be seen as punishments justly deserved.

Until the coming of Christ mankind had been ruled and guided by Divine Powers by whom the destinies of tribes and nations were ordered through the mediation of kings and priests—their representatives on earth. But since the time of Christ the way has been opened for each individual man increasingly to take on the guidance of his own destiny. This tremendous change meant that man no longer lived a life decreed by fate, a life in which everything was strictly ordained, bound by iron necessity which stemmed from consequences of his past; but that for the first time man was given the freedom to make his own decisions, to make atonement himself for his past shortcomings, no longer because he was bound to do so, but because he himself now accepted responsibility for his own actions and wished to make amends.

Christ, the Son of God, had descended to the earth to take upon Himself the sins of the world. Being innocent He suffered the undeserved agony of the crucifixion, and it was of His own free will that He submitted to the worst punishment, reserved by the customs of the time only for the lowest kind of criminal.

Reincarnation and Karma

For the redemption of mankind He offered Himself on the Cross to bear the sins committed by others—even the sins of the whole world.

When we human beings try to follow in the footsteps of Christ it even becomes possible, through Him, that out of love for our brother we are allowed to take on some portion of the burdens he bears as part of his destiny and which hinder his progress.

This, then, is one essential aspect of the complete transformation that was brought about by Christ; through the healing of this man who was blind from birth people's eyes could be opened to the realisation that the whole life of mankind and the earth was changed. No longer was the man's affliction to be understood in the light of ancient laws alone, for something quite new had entered on the scene and had completely altered the way such a case could be judged. Blindness in a child at birth had previously been seen as a consequence of sin committed in the past, but this man's blindness was different: it had come upon him not because he deserved punishment, but "that the works of God might be made manifest in him" and so, through him, people might become aware of the tremendous events that were taking place in their midst.

This can throw completely new light on the work we do in the present day with children who are afflicted from birth. There may indeed be those among them who suffer because of the sins of their forefathers, or whose illness is a consequence of their own sins and failures in earlier lives; but there are others, equally ill, whose condition is not part of their own destiny, who need not in fact have shouldered this burden, but have done so for the sake of helping others.

The old laws of destiny belonging to the times of the Old Testament did not, of course, altogether cease to exist with the coming of Christ; they continued to operate, and this was clearly stated by Jesus when He said: "Think not that I am come to destroy the law, or the prophets: I am not come to destroy, but to fulfil." (Matthew, 5.17.) But then He also said: "A new commandment I give unto you, That ye love one another; as I have loved you, that ye also love one another. By this shall all men know that ye are my disciples, if ye have love one to another." (John, 13.34.)

The verses immediately following this passage from the Gospel are most revealing. Simon Peter understands the meaning of Christ's words and wishes to follow Him; but Christ says: "Thou canst not follow me now; but thou shalt follow me afterwards. Peter said unto Him, Lord, why cannot I follow thee now? I will lay down my life for thy sake Jesus answered him, Wilt thou lay down thy life for my sake? Verily, verily, I say unto thee, the cock shall not crow, till thou hast denied me thrice."

Peter has understood, but it is a far cry from understanding what needs to be done and being able to do it. Peter thinks that he is ready to lay down his life for Christ's sake, but Christ knows him better than he knows himself. There is still that in Peter which causes him—only a short time afterwards—to deny his Lord three times. Only many years later was Peter ready to act by the new commandment, to follow in the footsteps of Christ and lay down his life for the Lord. It takes time, therefore, even where there is good will, to fulfil the old laws by carrying them further in the light of the new commandment. The old lingers on with the new and people who still abide exclusively by the old laws live side by side with individuals who, like Simon Peter, have understood and won through to fulfil the new commandment. Christ Himself forces no one to follow Him but waits patiently till people are ready to do so of their own accord.

The fact that the Christian faith was subsequently spread by the sword, that religious wars have been fought in the name of Christ, and dogmas have been set up which make people unfree—all this was due to lack of understanding by the followers of Christ who interpreted His message in the light of the old Covenant. Christ came to lead people out of the bondage of the old into the freedom of the future but it is part even of this freedom that it can be gained only when man accepts it freely. Addressing Himself to the people around Him, Christ said: You have asked the question; I will give you the answer "if you will receive it"—or "if you will accept it".

So it happens that two thousand years after Christ we find people who have accepted Christ's teaching and people who have not; some have begun to understand, others have not, and there is as yet no one who has understood *fully* the message of Christianity. So vast, so complex is this message that it will take humanity "till the end of the earthly days" to realise fully, not only the *teaching* of Christ, but *His Deed* for mankind which was done through His death and resurrection.

When we begin to consider all these things in connection with the afflicted children and resolve to try and put them into practice and apply them to the manifold situations these children present to us we shall surely stand in wonder and amazement before the richness and infinite variety of experience which meets us in human karma. We can only feel very humble towards the wisdom of the universe and the great lessons that life itself can teach us. One thing becomes immediately very clear: that it is far from easy to form a true judgement of the mentally afflicted child who stands before us. It is difficult enough to assess the ordinary, normal person; it may be years before we really come to know a person and only then because some particular event brings to light qualities we had never suspected in him; with exceptional children it is even more difficult: because of their defects and handicaps, the moments when we are able to catch a glimpse of their true personality are rare. Indeed such moments may not occur in a whole lifetime and then these people will continue to remain as strangers in our midst.

Reference was made in an earlier chapter to the many different factors which may lie behind an inability to speak, for example. This applies equally to everything else in life. A child may be backward because his development is still to be begun; or he may be backward because of things he himself did which caused him to lose capacities he had once possessed; again it could be that his progress has been hindered by others; lastly, he may be in a situation similar to the man who was born blind—that is to say he may have taken on his affliction voluntarily for the sake of helping others. We therefore need to examine very carefully our relationship to a handicapped person with whom we are connected.

In speaking of these things it must be remembered that we are attempting to describe in earthly language something which is of a spiritual nature and for which, therefore, no adequate earthly words can be found. If, for instance, we speak of a personality "giving" or "sharing" with another, or again if we were to refer to an individual "choosing" certain people who can help or be helped by him on earth, it is almost bound to sound very banal. But this "choosing" for example, would not be the kind we do on earth when one chooses a certain garment to wear or a partner at a dance, but it is more in the nature of an impulse—a potential. One might say, for example, that the impulse of electricity is always to travel to earth and it is more in this way that the human individual before birth—formed, as he is, by the experiences and human connections of former lives on earth—has within him an impulse, which not only draws him back to begin a new life on earth, but at the same time leads him to seek, as it were, certain people and situations which are necessary for his own development and that of others.

If it is possible for an individual to take on some part of another person's destiny, it must be equally possible to share gifts and capacities with one to whom we may be indebted or who is otherwise closely connected with us. It is conceivable from this point of view that the brilliantly clever brother, or sister, of a backward child could owe many of his outstanding gifts to a sacrifice made for him by the backward member of the family—a sacrifice that was made even before they were born. Of course it is not so in *every* case but it is worth considering and the mere fact of serious consideration will surely bring about a significant change in our attitude towards any member of our family who may be handicapped. We shall no longer feel angry, impatient or embittered that he is not as bright and capable as we are, nor shall we be so proud of our own abilities; for it may well be we have these gifts because another person's share has been added to ours, because someone has renounced for our sake certain possibilities for himself during this present life. We need not feel such a thought as an obligation, or in any way binding upon us, but it is good to have it in our consciousness as an open question. The possibility is just as real as the possibility we have of helping another person in the material realm by putting money or goods at his disposal. The amount a friend can spare for a time may be just what a person needs to enable him to do something worth while for the benefit of others as well as himself. It means that the giver is poorer for a time than he need have been, but as we would never say of a generous friend who gives away money: "Poor man, he cannot afford much" so with a handicapped child we can never be justified in saying: "Poor child, he will never come to much; he is not worth bothering about." For all we know many of the blessings we enjoy in life may be due to him or to another like him; therefore to offer as much help as we can to these children, at the same time endeavouring to make the most of our own gifts, is the least we can do. Far from binding us, however, these things should make us realise with deep gratitude how wonderfully interlinked all our destinies are.

While we are speaking of this whole theme of sacrifice for the sake of another it will be good to think also of that most heart-rending experience which many parents have to face: the death of their child. We have already spoken of Simon Peter's words: "Lord–I will lay down my life for thy sake" and it is in the light of these words that we should contemplate even the death of a young child; for it may well be that they have indeed "laid down their life" for our sake. Again it is not, of course, always so and there may be quite other reasons for an early death. That is something we cannot know or judge with our earthly consciousness. Such profound decisions belong in the realm of human destiny; the answers to our questions are not to be found through intellectual knowledge, they are in a quite different region and live in far deeper layers of man's being.

There is one other aspect we should consider when a life has been cut short in childhood. When we study the history of mankind we know that there have always been millions of ordinary people with average gifts, but among them we also find certain personalities of quite outstanding talent. In every century there have been such individuals who stand out from the crowd. Usually such people have been far ahead of their time, and have achieved great deeds for the benefit of all mankind. When we read the biographies of such people we can only wonder how they found strength to accomplish so much. We marvel at their energy and endurance, their understanding and foresight, so far beyond the capacities of any ordinary person. It may well be that such individualities have been long preparing for that important life task, by storing up in a previous life, or lives, the very forces they received from those who loved and cared for them. If each succeeding century in history is to bring progress for the human race, the individualities who are destined to carry mankind forward to each new stage of development must be specially equipped to meet their task. The abundance of life forces and the extraordinary, almost superhuman capacities of such historic personalities cannot be explained by heredity alone. Seen only in the context of one life on earth, the phenomenon of their existence remains inexplicable, but when it is set against the background of reincarnation then we can begin to understand, however dimly, what is at work in the shaping of human destiny, in the making of history, and realise that the death of a young child—which is often so difficult for us to understand—may also be part of the great mysteries of Karma.

CHAPTER XII

... *Now Christmas Can Come*

In this concluding chapter, I shall speak mainly of one patient, whose life and conduct has taught a great deal to those who have worked with him over the years. He has lived in the

Stanley Slater (Mops)
24-12-1924 – 1-2-1997

Home-School I have been trying to describe since he was a small boy and though he is now a man he remains in many ways a child. In his own way he knows many things and he ponders deeply on all that happens in the life around him. He remembers, for instance, the birthdays of almost every person who has ever lived and worked in the Home, children as well as adults, and he keeps a watchful eye on all that goes on. He does not like people to go away, for then the family is incomplete. So when anyone announces cheerfully that he is going on holiday, this young man asks sadly: "When are you coming back again?" He also gets very worried if people are ill, for in his opinion it is wrong and bad to be ill. Everyone should be well and so if he hears that someone is in bed he enquires anxiously: "When will he be getting up again?" When he himself is not well he does his utmost to hide it and tries never to show any pain for fear of being sent to bed—for he thinks that to be ill means to be naughty and being sent to bed is, for him, a punishment.

This patient finds it very difficult to communicate and make people understand what is in his mind. At first sight he appears confused, yet in a deeper sense he is not really so. He is very well aware of what goes on around him and in his anxiety that all should be well seems to feel a deep responsibility for everything and everyone. For instance, not a day passes without his going round to inspect every corner of the large buildings, to satisfy himself that all is in order. He always seems to know if an important conversation is taking place: soon after the talk has begun—sometimes even before—a door will open quietly and he will appear—eavesdropping as it were: yet this is not just idle curiosity on his part but a deep concern for all that is connected with the life of the Home.

Outwardly there seems little he could do personally to set things right if they go wrong—yet one has a real feeling of protection when he is around. To all who have lived with him it has become obvious that, in spite of all his handicaps, this is a great person, one who knows many things and who is well able to think, though unable to express his meaning.

He is one of many patients whose condition makes it quite

clear that it is not the brain that produces the thinking but that the brain is merely the instrument needed to translate the content of thinking into the forms of thought, which can then be expressed in language through which the human being is able to communicate and share his thoughts with others. The human thinking is an invisible and purely spiritual activity which, through the functioning of the brain, can be made manifest in the material world, from which however it does not originate. Although it is not the matter of the brain which produces the thinking, naturally if the instrument is impaired, if the brain is injured or not properly developed, the thought-forming ability is unable to show itself. This is one reason why people believe that thinking itself arises from the brain and can have no existence at all when there is not a brain to produce it. In reality it is quite the reverse: it is the thinking which has created its instrument the brain, and equally all the other mental faculties of man have fashioned and formed the organs they need for their physical expression, making use of the qualities and behaviour of matter to achieve this end. For instance, man puts his brain at the service of his thinking ability by making use of the fluid processes in his body. The rhythmical flow and movement of fluids, the living rise and fall of the cerebral spinal fluid, lend to the brain the weightlessness without which it could not function. Similarly it is the respiratory processes in man's organism which enable him to manifest his life of feelings and emotions; and because he lives in the experiences of cold and warmth man is able to develop and use his powers of will. We see therefore that these three elements of water, air and fire are vehicles which enable man to exercise his mental faculties, but they do not produce them.

 The human brain can be likened to a musical instrument. A player cannot give a good performance on a broken violin however great his musical ability. The violin is essential to make the music audible, but it does not produce the music nor the musician: these exist independently of the instrument. There are a great many patients whose instrument of the brain does

The Exceptional Child

Violet Long, Shirley Hutchins, John Lawrence, Kalmia Bittleston, Maria Geuter Peter Donald Eliot, Stanley
Sunfield, Selly, Oak c1932-3

Stanley dressed as a waiter with the Kitchen Saff at the opening of the Pottery 1938 at Sunfield, Clent.

... Now Christmas Can Come

*The Boys' House 1947
Sunfield, Clent*

*Stanley Aug. 1948
Sunfield, Clent*

The Exceptional Child

not function properly, therefore they cannot express their thoughts. But this does not of necessity mean that they cannot think. The incident that I shall now relate will perhaps make this clearer. It concerns the same adult patient I have been describing and it will bring us at the same time to where we began in the first chapter: to the season of Christmas.

Again the festival of Christmas was approaching and during the weeks of Advent it was noticed that the young man was always missing at lunch time. He would disappear just as the meal began and only turned up when it was almost finished. Asked where he had been and why he was so late he would give no answer. Telling him that he would have to miss the meal altogether if he was late again had no effect; sure enough when lunch time came round he would be missing.

One day I went in search of him and when I found him he was standing at the open door of the theatre, gazing across to the stage. He stood there lost in a dream and did not hear me coming, so I was able to watch him for a while. The previous evening there had been a rehearsal of the Nativity Play which the staff perform for the children every year on Christmas Eve. The stage curtains were open and the stage itself was still set for the scene of the Christmas play: the stable in Bethlehem, the crib with straw and hay, the branches of fir and the great gold star. As the man stood in the doorway happily gazing at all this from afar, he smiled and I heard him murmur to himself: "It's all right—they are doing it—look at it—it's all there—they have not forgotten—Christmas can come now—Christmas can come!"

When he became aware of my presence he tried to slip away knowing that he had again missed the beginning of the meal and would be frowned upon for being late. I assured him that I was not cross with him, but would just like to know what he was doing. Then he told me his secret, in confidence, and repeated what I had already heard him saying to himself. Why, I asked him, did he always choose lunch time to come here. I felt very stupid when he gave me his answer; he said quite simply: "Because there is nobody here at lunch time—they are all in the dining room."

This man had been in the Home for most of his life and so had experienced the festivals of the seasons many times; in his own way he had come to know the deep significance of Christmas.

All children love Christmas and many have their own personal reasons for looking forward to it—as the little "Donkey" did. It is essentially the children's festival and the main festival of the year; but this handicapped man had been able to see even more deeply. There is an inner pathway of progress which leads us through the celebration of the Twelve Days of Christmas from the birth of the Child on Christmas Eve—the birth of the human Child Jesus—to Epiphany which is the Day of the Baptism by John in Jordan and is thus the birth day of the Son of God in the human being—the birth of Christ in the Man Jesus. For this handicapped man it had become of supreme importance that the Twelve Days of Christmas should be celebrated in the true and proper way, that again the road might be open for every human being to follow in the footsteps of Christ and bring to birth in himself the Divine Principle. This is what St. Paul speaks of when he says: "Not I but Christ in me." Every human being, whether he be normal or handicapped, is subject to the Fall. Man was created in the Image of God but this image has been impaired and darkened in all of us because we have descended more deeply into the realm of matter than was originally ordained. A handicapped person may be more aware of this "darkening of the Image of God" even than a normal person, for behind him too, in spite of his temporary defects and shortcomings, there stands his higher self still unimpaired—his eternal spiritual individuality. It is only from that realm that light can begin to shine once more into man's darkness, that true help for the future can come to him.

This handicapped man has chosen to have his own birthday on Christmas Eve and his inner eye is always searching for that goal which is connected with the Day of Epiphany. Therefore it is essential for him that the people around him should

The Exceptional Child

stand beside him in mutual striving for a true understanding of these things, that they should learn to find—for him, and with him—the inner pathway that leads from the experience of Christmas Eve to the experience of Epiphany.

In his present condition as a handicapped person, the picture this man presents is of one who has made a great sacrifice, one who has bound himself with his own hands in order to lend his precious faculties to others, in the hope that, through being as he is, he can help to open their eyes to what is happening in their midst—even as the man in the Gospel bore his blindness, not because he deserved it, or because his parents had sinned, but that through him "the works of God might be made manifest". Thus we find this man today waiting and watching, like a guardian angel, to ensure that the true spirit of Christmas and Epiphany can find a home in the hearts of men:

"Look—it is all there—they are doing it—now Christmas can come!"

How To Help Your Growing Child
Through an Understanding of the Four Temperaments in Childhood

Part I

THE NEED FOR SOUND KNOWLEDGE

Many parents today are worried about their children. The fact is that children seldom choose to be the ideal little people their parents would wish them to be. But, apart from this, even when parents love their children as they are, there are too often symptoms in the child's behaviour and constitution which cause serious anxiety to those responsible for their upbringing and their future.

Parents who are worried in this way are usually keen to make contact with people who have had to deal with similar situations. They are eager to hear the experiences of others, in order to avoid mistakes which have already been made and to benefit from helpful ideas which have already been tried out and proved to be successful.

Often enough parents discover that there are as many different remedies for their particular troubles as there are people ready to give advice. Some people will make them fear the worst for their child unless something is done immediately; others may fill them with hope that the particular difficulty which they perceive in their child is "just one of those many phases," which nearly all children have to pass through at one time or another, and that the trouble will eventually settle itself if not too much weight is attached to it.

In such circumstances—as indeed in any other difficult situation of life—people are led again and again to realise that the one and only remedy which can help is a real, sound *knowledge* of the problem involved.

We feel, and rightly so, that our children are too precious to become the objects of experiment—experiment which, in any event, may turn out unfavourably. True and sound knowledge alone can support us in our justified and helpless anxiety; it alone can dissolve our unnecessary alarm and furnish us with the calm strength which comes from the certainty of knowing what to do and being able to do it.

Part I
THE FOUR TEMPERAMENTS

An important key to the understanding of the problems which arise in connection with the education of children, both in school and at home, is the knowledge of the Four Temperaments.

This knowledge is as old as the hills but, like so many other treasures of ancient wisdom, it has been forgotten and pushed into the background. The gigantic wealth of scientific discoveries of the past four centuries, the satisfaction in the achievement of new knowledge, and the pride of progress—these have all turned the minds of men to discard the knowledge of earlier centuries as being childish and utterly insufficient. This has meant that in many cases, precious stones have been thrown away along with the dead rock.

We owe it to the work of the late Rudolf Steiner that much of the ancient wisdom of man has become available to us again, not in the way in which it lived among the peoples of olden times, but in an entirely new and more conscious way such as accords with the modern mind.

The methods of Rudolf Steiner's spiritual research are the methods of natural science and, in a strictly scientific way, he has been able to penetrate the laws of world-evolution and of the evolution of Mankind. Taking into account all the achievements of our own age, he has carried human knowledge forward into new fields, and in doing so has made the otherwise unintelligible writings of earlier centuries transparent for the understanding of the scientifically trained intellect of today.

Instead of discarding true knowledge of bygone days, we find we have to re-learn and re-form it, developing it further in a way which is in keeping with the standard of this century. At the same time, the way lies open for new discoveries and new work for centuries to come. The knowledge of the Four Temperaments is, so to speak, only one chapter—but a very important chapter—in the vast, living book of knowledge which Rudolf Steiner has given to those who want to work towards a sound and healing education for our children.

The Four Temperaments have always been known as the Sanguine, the Choleric, the Phlegmatic and the Melancholic. In order to illustrate what is meant by these four terms, allow me to use a picture which, though perhaps showing the humorous side of the subject will, I hope, also serve to stress the danger points.

Imagine that, during the night, a terrible gale has been blowing; a great tree has been uprooted and has fallen directly across a lane, completely blocking the way.

THE SANGUINE TEMPERAMENT

Now imagine that a sanguine person is the first to arrive on the scene and to find his path barred by the fallen tree. He will be thrilled at the exciting newness of an unforeseen situation. His adventurous spirit will at once be roused and will prompt him to look at each detail with great interest—to find out how and why it happened, how much damage has been done, etc. But all this lively interest will not serve the object of finding out what might be done to clear up the mess; nor will the fallen tree prove an obstacle to him in pursuing his path, once his curiosity has been satisfied.

He will simply climb or jump over the tree with the greatest ease. Should he stumble and fall in the process or carry off a few bruises and scratches, or soil and tear his clothes, he will not mind very much; for scratches will heal and bruises will not hurt for ever, while soiled clothes can easily be washed and a few holes can surely be mended. After all, he feels it only right that he should pay for such an exciting adventure; so he will skip along, telling anyone he meets about the fascinating discovery he has made, about the strength of the gale, the huge size of the tree, etc., and he will be only too happy in the unexpected entertainment which has fallen in his way.

THE CHOLERIC TEMPERAMENT

But suppose a choleric person discovers the fallen tree. His fiery nature will immediately be roused, and he will feel himself challenged by the obstacle which has dared to lie in his path. He will not think twice, but in a second his sleeves will be rolled up and, with flashing eyes, he will set his whole concentrated energy against the weighty mass of the fallen giant. In his rage he will not stop to consider that it is perhaps none of his business to interfere, nor that he may do more harm than good if he attempts such a task single-handed. He will be conscious only of one thing: the tree is in his way and must be moved!

Impetuously he will procure or improvise tools, probably taking what he needs without asking permission of the owner, and should the implements prove too weak and fragile for the job, this will not deter him; when one breaks he will cast it aside impatiently and take up another. That he may damage the hedges which border the lane or that the owner of the tree may have quite other plans about how it should be cut up and used, these are things which will not occur to him, and if the owner turns up later and complains about the matter, our choleric will march away like a thundercloud, grumbling loudly about the stupidity and ingratitude of people who don't know a good piece of work when they see it! So, he will go to work blindly, regardless of the ruin he will leave behind him, and equally regardless of his own person, never stopping until he stands like a victor on a battlefield, viewing his work with the greatest satisfaction.

THE PHLEGMATIC TEMPERAMENT

Now let us consider the reactions of a phlegmatic when faced with a similar situation. He will approach the tree at a comfortable pace, and will slowly take in the fact that the way appears to be blocked in front of him. All the same, he will proceed quietly until he is quite close to the tree, for there *may* after all be a way of squeezing through without the effort of climbing over or removing the obstacle, which would save him a lot of trouble. Having arrived at the place, therefore, he will take his time and will make a careful survey of the situation. Gradually he will arrive at the conclusion that things are as he feared, and that the road is completely blocked. His whole experience (carefully tried and tested over a long period) will tell him that this tree is not likely to move out of his way of its own accord, so after great deliberation he will eventually come to the conclusion that the easiest and wisest course will be himself to move out of the way of the tree. Upon this decision, he will slowly turn back and proceed by another road, which he fervently hopes will not be blocked before he arrives at his destination.

THE MELANCHOLIC TEMPERAMENT

Finally let us turn to the person of melancholic temperament and see how he deals with the difficulty. For him, the event will not seem so entirely strange and unexpected. Such things have happened to him so many times before. So he will stand before the obstacle, utterly crestfallen, apparently quite unable to do anything whatever about the situation in which he finds himself through no fault of his own. His whole being will be plunged into a vast sea of unutterable misery.

He will stand with arms hanging and for a long time he will wonder why on earth it must happen that he *alone* of all people should have to suffer this undeserved misfortune of finding such an obstacle in his path. Just for once he had made up his mind to take a really enjoyable walk, and *of course,* something was bound to go wrong. He will feel quite helpless and God-forsaken and will not for a long while be so ready again to set out for a country walk! For many days afterwards he will continue to ponder deeply over his own personal, everlasting misfortunes, which follow him everywhere.

In these pictures I have tried to give a description of the entirely different reactions of four people to the same situation. In each of the four cases described, one of the Temperaments is predominant. Naturally, in between such pure examples of one-sided temperament, we shall find among our children an endless variety of mixtures, when two or three, or even all four temperaments are combined.

Part I
UNDERSTANDING THE CHILD

If we learn to know the symptoms of each temperament as they come to expression in the child's features, in his build, his walk, the colour of his hair, in his reactions to life—the way he eats, sleeps and behaves generally—and if we are also able to learn how to deal with the different temperaments, we shall be able to help the children to find a balance and to avoid these extremes. Then we shall no longer stand helpless before a child, whatever difficulties we may perceive.

We shall not be discouraged by the child who will not take anything seriously and who finds it impossible to concentrate. We shall not be daunted by the child who flings himself into violent tempers on the least provocation. We shall not lose patience with the slow, lazy and dull child who cannot be bothered to learn anything. Nor shall we allow ourselves to become unduly depressed by the child who is entirely preoccupied with his own shortcomings, who will not mix easily with other children, and who is inclined to suffer from an inferiority complex.

Many difficulties, great and small, can be overcome and the children can be helped enormously if we, the grown-ups who are responsible for their well-being and their healthy development, will try to gain, in the first place, a clear knowledge of the problems which confront us.

Part II

WHY FOUR TEMPERAMENTS?

In the previous chapter I tried to give a picture of the way in which each temperament might react in a given situation. Now let us turn to the question: Why do we speak of four temperaments? Is it just by chance that, in human behaviour, four kinds of reaction towards the outer circumstances of life can be observed? Let us try to look at the problem in an unprejudiced way.

Every human being lives in a body, but this body is not *himself;* it is really only like a house in which he lives. When someone is fast asleep his body is there in front of me, but *he* is not there for me to talk to.

The human body is composed of solid substances the hardest of which are the teeth; it contains a large percentage of fluids which are in constant rhythmical movement; it is permeated by air, through the breathing process of lungs and skin; and it has an average temperature, which varies in different parts of the organism and which can rise or fall in case of illness.

The soul dwells within this body and each has a strong influence upon the other. Fear can make us feel cold and can cause our body to tremble; shame can drive the blood to our cheeks; and anxiety can alter the rhythm of the heart-beat. On the other hand a disturbed digestion can cause depression in the soul and a certain disease of the heart may be the reason for great restlessness of mind.

The child is infinitely more dependent on the comfort or discomfort of his body than the grownup person who can make a conscious effort to overcome weaknesses. When a child shows difficulties such as restlessness or inactivity, violent tempers or inferiority complexes, this may not be entirely the fault of the child, but may be due to disturbances between the different functions of his organism There should be a healthy balance in the child's body between the formation of solid substance the

Part II

rhythmical movement of fluids, the process of breathing, and the production of just the right temperature. This balance of the physical parts will in turn be the foundation for a harmonious balance of all four temperaments in the life of the soul.

As mentioned before, in many children there is a happy mixture of two, three, or even all four temperaments. But it can happen that the processes which build up the *solid* matter of the body are too strong; the child will then be overpowered by the hardening forces in his bones, he will develop fixed ideas in his mind, and a melancholic temperament will arise. A child who is too much aware of the movements of *fluids* within his body will be phlegmatic. The restlessness of the sanguine child is due to his living too strongly within the element of *air,* and the hot tempers of a choleric are the result of the child being overpowered by the *heat* processes of his own body.

FINDING A BALANCE

Anxiety for the child's healthy development begins only when one temperament is present in a one-sided and exaggerated form. Wherever we see one temperament predominating to an alarming extent, it becomes our responsibility to do all we can to help the child to establish a balance before it is too late and he has become set in his course. Now let us look more closely at each temperament, examples of which have already been given in Chapter I where we described the incident of the fallen tree.

The sanguine temperament belongs to childhood as the phlegmatic temperament belongs to old age. Even a melancholic person can show traces of sanguinity during childhood. It is this temperament which lends wings to the soul. Life on earth lies before a child like a fairyland as yet unexplored, full of hidden wonders and beauties. The carefree happiness of childhood which dances like a butterfly from blossom to blossom is granted to us but once in a life-time, and we should guard it for our children as something infinitely precious. In his play the child takes his first steps toward the skill and wisdom of his later years. In this sense every child has the right to be sanguine up to a point, to skip and dance from adventure to adventure, to be interested in everything, to ask questions about everything We should take great care that our answers never close and seal a matter. They should be given in such a way that they can lead to deeper and greater questions in later life.

DANGER OF THE SANGUINE TEMPERAMENT

The danger of the sanguine temperament begins when lively interest in everything turns into a restlessness which loses all direction. This happened in the case of little Joyce. She was a pretty child with blue eyes, fair curls and a cheeky little turned-up nose. She was small for her age, light-footed and slender like a fairy. Everyone was fond of her and she was fond of everyone, but her affections were neither deep nor lasting. As she grew older a certain carelessness and superficiality became more and more apparent. She was bright and intelligent, would quickly understand what she was taught but just as quickly forget it again. She would cheerfully begin at once on any given task and abandon it unfinished with the easiest conscience in the world. One day in school, when copying from the blackboard, she turned all her letter M's into L's and all her R's into T's, etc. When the teacher found that all her writing had gone wrong, Joyce said cheerfully: "Oh, I know! But the letters were tired of always looking the same. They wanted a change!"

For Joyce it would be a real blessing if someone who loved her and understood her could succeed in capturing her fleeting affections, so that they could grow towards a genuine love which would be a stable element in her life. For the sake of someone whom she loved deeply she would bring herself to finish many an abandoned task and thus steady herself again a temperament which constantly runs away with her. She needs the company of someone who not only lives up to her speed in changing the subject, but who can even make it difficult for her to catch up with him; someone who can hold her in suspense, who can play unexpected tricks on her, so that she never quite knows where she is with him nor foresee what is going to happen next. She needs games which force her to be more than sanguine in order not to miss the point; for after a period of such breathtaking play, which does full justice to their temperament, sanguine children have often been only too ready to sit quite still for a while and listen to a story or concentrate on a picture book. Such periods of utter quiet could gradually be increased and lengthened; they would be like healing balm to the restless soul of such a child and would give her one safe rock to cling to when in danger of being swept off her feet.

The child's parents need to be very wise in thinking of ever new ways to satisfy their little girl's need for variety. But great care should be taken to ensure that all changes and surprises happen within a framework of the utmost regularity. For Joyce's sake one should insist on the strictest discipline in regard to meals, rest-times, walks, etc. These daily occurrences should happen with the unquestionable precision of a sunrise or a sunset, and should stand for the child like pillars in the whirl of passing events. Thus the instability of Joyce's temperament could be met with an external steadiness which would prove to be a valuable inner support to her in later years.

TREATMENT OF THE CHOLERIC CHILD

Roger was very different from Joyce. He offered the purest example of a choleric temperament; he gave the impression of being a little volcano ready to erupt at any moment. There was a hidden fire burning within him, an accumulated strength which would either find release in a violent outburst of temper or spend itself on some enormous task which he would try to tackle. Even when quite a little boy he would pursue his aims with grim determination and would not give in until he had got what he wanted. His mother soon learned from bitter experience that she could do nothing at all with him if she lost her temper and reacted irritably. The fact that for the sake of her child she made enormous efforts of self-control was perhaps the most effective help Roger received in his earlier years.

A choleric person is always determined to assert his own will. He knows his aim and never doubts his power to achieve it. Therefore, a choleric child will accept the guidance only of someone whom he can admire. He will recognise our right to teach him only if we can prove that we know what we are talking about and that we are capable of achieving a great deal more than we can do as yet. We lose his esteem at once if we allow him to spot any of our weak points.

In fact, we cannot educate a choleric child unless we ourselves constantly practise self-control and self-education.* We shall do well if we allow him as much as possible to be in the company of people whom he can admire and we should always give him tasks which are just a little beyond him. This will make him use his energy and strong will in a helpful way, instead of having to find release in destructive outbursts of temper.

---

*See "Knowledge of the Higher Worlds " by Rudolf Steiner (Rudolf Steiner Press, London)." Understanding Our Fellow Men" by Knud Asbjorn Lund, and " Hygiene of the Soul" by Dr. F. W. Zeylmans van Emmichoven (New Knowledge Books, London).

Part III

TREATMENT OF THE PHLEGMATIC CHILD

Having spoken of the sanguine and choleric temperaments, let us now consider the phlegmatic. As an example we will take a little girl named Bertha, who is so phlegmatic that her parents have become extremely worried about her.

As a baby she was easy to look after, for she was quite content to lie for hours at a time in her pram or cot. The only thing she seemed to be really interested in was food, and this she demanded at regular intervals. The anxiety of her parents began when the time came for Bertha to learn to sit up, to walk and to speak, for she was slow to the extent of backwardness. Then her parents began to look for advice and were anxious to do all in their power to help their little girl.

It is obvious that Bertha's one aim in life is to be left in peace, so that she can give herself fully to the enjoyments of sleeping, eating and digesting. She is all too comfortable inside her fat little body, which is like a cushion between her and the world. For her the happiest times of the day are the hours just after a big meal when she will let herself sink dreamily into satisfied feelings of well-being. Every wish for mental or physical activity seems to be drowned in the flow of her digestive processes. If she is left to her own devices she will develop no interest in life beyond the comfort of her own body.

Such a child should not be given too much food which fattens or is too easily digested. Her whole condition will improve if she is prevented from getting too fat. Puddings, cakes, cocoa, fat soups, etc., should be avoided if possible. She needs fresh fruit and vegetables, and things like nuts and crusts which require a certain amount of chewing. Her desire for food will at least stir her into the activity of obtaining it, and it will do her good to bite into plenty of hard apples.

It is important also to see that Bertha does not sleep too long. She should of course have the amount of sleep which is reasonable for a child of her age, but she should not be allowed to lie in bed indefinitely, just because she is too lazy to get up. Nor is it good for such a child to be left too much alone. The more she can be persuaded to join in the games of other children the better it will be for her. It will help her too if the grown-ups will frequently play games with her, such as "This little piggie went to Market," or to let her ride on their knee to the rhythm of a little verse or song, and dropping her down suddenly at the last word or line.

Such games—and there are many different ones—are excellent for waking up such sleepy children. All through the steady and almost monotonous first part of the game, there runs the anticipation of the one moment when, suddenly something else will happen. The children know exactly what is coming and when to expect it, and yet ever again it takes them by surprise when it does happen. There are also games where there is no verse or song to lead up to the moment of excitement. The children know that it is coming, but they do not know when, and they become brightly alert in order not to be caught napping. With games like "Snap" or "Happy Families" they have to be constantly "on the spot" or they will miss their chance. Other games begin very slowly and sleepily and gradually accelerate to such an extent that, with shouts of laughter, the children break down simply because they cannot keep up the speed. Any game of this kind is excellently suited to rouse phlegmatic children from their apathy.

HANDLING THE MELANCHOLIC CHILD

There remains now the melancholic temperament to be considered. Little James was easily the most melancholic child I ever met. Although his body was of slender build, it appeared to be too heavy for him. He walked with dragging step, his head bent, his shoulders rounded. As mentioned above, the melancholic temperament arises when the hardening powers which build the skeleton becomes too strong and begin to overstep the limits of their lawful realm. They are good and beneficial for us as long as they give the right amount of firmness to our bones and teeth; but they become wrong and harmful when they are active outside their proper sphere, producing such illnesses as gall-stones, rheumatism, gout, constipation, etc. It is their task to harden the child's skeleton sufficiently for him to be upright and learn to walk. But in the case of the melancholic child they go beyond the point of establishing the necessary support; they densify further and become a weight upon the child.

In the normal course of development the hardening powers work more strongly in an old person than in a child, whose bones are still comparatively soft. This is the reason why James so often behaves like a little grown-up. He lacks the carefree happiness of childhood and takes everything much too seriously. He has great, sad eyes set in a pale little face, and he is capable of suffering and sorrow much beyond his age.

Two things this child needs above all; warmth and sweetness. He needs the inner warmth of love and understanding, and he needs the outer warmth of really protective clothing–even more than other children do. A melancholic child on a cold winter's day wearing cotton ankle socks has not much hope of feeling more kindly disposed towards a world which, in any case, offers him little comfort. We shall make his condition worse if we try to harden him against cold, by giving him cold baths for instance. In him, the hardening forces are already all too strong, in fact they are his whole trouble. Besides having a hardening effect a cold bath is always a shock to the system, even in the case of grown-ups who can anticipate the shock and enjoy it.

There would be far less rheumatism and gout in the world if the habit of hardening oneself through cold baths were not so widespread. We literally harden substances in the joints which should remain fluid. A phlegmatic child who, in any case, lives too much in the fluid element of his body and likes to swim in vague ideas, may benefit from a cold splash and an occasional gentle shock–it will pull him together and increase his consciousness. To a melancholic child however a shock of any kind acts like poison and will make him shut up like an oyster. We want such a child to open out and unburden his depressed little mind; we want him to gain confidence in other people. So we defeat our own ends if we allow him to have more shocks than life already provides for him.

Sufficient warmth may not be as difficult to provide as the necessary sweetness—especially in these days. All the same the mother of a melancholic child should make sure that he always has his full share of sugar and sweets and perhaps even a little extra if it can be managed. A melancholic child will be more than grateful to know that someone has made a little sacrifice for his sake. Just as he can never forget a hurt, so will he never forget a kindness.

But we must be careful not to spoil him. Melancholic people are always too inclined to be thinking of themselves. Therefore, the child should never be made to feel that he is *entitled* to more sugar and sweets than others—but the fact remains that he *needs* more.

CONSIDER EACH CHILD INDIVIDUALLY

To be " fair" to children does not mean to give them all an equal share of everything. What is good for one child may be quite harmful for another. For instance, it is downright bad for an over-sanguine child to have too much sugar. When dealing with children it naturally requires great tact on the part of the grown-ups to see that each has what he needs and what is good for him, yet without creating envy or ill-feeling among them. It can be done however, and we should make the effort to consider each child individually.

We shall never persuade a melancholic child to forget his troubles by trying to amuse him. We have to take into account the fact that he really loves to be sad. Such children go out of their way to look for trouble, and it is our task to transform their fundamental sadness into a positive strength.

Part III
THE EFFECTS OF RIGHT AND WRONG HANDLING

Rudolf Steiner has often drawn attention to the fact that we can help a child only if we work with the qualities which he actually possesses. We do great harm to him if we merely try to eradicate his faults, and we harm him equally much if we try to inject qualities into him which we ourselves might wish him to possess, but which are alien to his nature. We should always accept a child as he is, with all his individual qualities, and then for his sake try to direct them into the right channels.

Without the proper guidance during childhood a sanguine person can lose all stability in life and live perpetually in golden dreams of the future which he will not have the strength to achieve. Phlegmatic and choleric people live, both of them, wrongly in the present; the one tending towards a dullness of mind which will make him content to leave things for ever as they are, the other tending towards a fanaticism which will be wanting to change the world continually, whether for good or ill. Lastly, the melancholic will live for ever in the past, never being able to leave it behind.

IN CONCLUSION

If guided rightly however, a sanguine person can bring such freshness and buoyancy to life that he can inspire others with ever new ideas and in any desperate situation he will be able to find a golden ray of hope which can lead him further.

A person who has been helped in childhood to overcome the dangers of his phlegma will be the most reliable friend, who will never fail in his duty and will be a calm and faithful stand-by in stormy weather.

A choleric who has learned to tame his fanatic impulses will be able to lend every ounce of his tremendous energy and strength of will to a good cause and help it through to success.

A melancholic child may grow up to become an excellent doctor or nurse, or to work in some other capacity where he can give comfort and relief to others. Just because he has had to battle with his own melancholic temperament, such a person will be able to bring to the tasks of life a specially deep understanding and compassion for the destiny of others.

Thus a knowledge of the Four Temperaments can be an enormous help to all of us who want to guide the children who are in our care along the right way in life.

Supplement

Euthanasia and Rudolf Steiner's Curative Education

Our friend and teacher, Miss Ursula Grahl, has been asked on frequent occasions to speak on the subject of Rudolf Steiner and Curative Education. Accordingly, at the 1955 Annual General Meeting, she delivered the following address, which we give to you as an outstanding contribution to the work of Curative Education. – An extract from THE JOURNAL OF THE THREE ROSES *Autumn, 1955 Vol. 1 No. 7*

Dear Friends,

...The Curative Education Course was given to people who had known Rudolf Steiner for some time. They themselves had had the impulse to begin the work of looking after and educating children who were in need of special care, and they had asked Rudolf Steiner to give them his advice on this matter, because they had come to recognise more and more that he was the one person who could give essential help. Rudolf Steiner had spent his whole life in opening up new ways of approach to Spiritual Science, which answers the needs of modern mankind, and the people who were permitted to take part in the lecture course on Curative Education had all had plenty of opportunity to experience the help which Anthroposophy offers in all situations and in all spheres of life. First of all, they had come to know Rudolf Steiner's philosophy, and they had found that this philosophy was able, more than any other world conception, to throw light upon the many great riddles of life. Moreover they had had occasions to witness that this philosophy was no mere theory, but was capable of dealing with the practical needs of everyday life. Schools had been opened which were based on Rudolf Steiner's ideas on education, and already the beneficial effect of such an education was apparent in many children; agriculturists had started to run farms according to the methods indicated by Rudolf Steiner, and results were beginning to show; doctors of medicine had become interested and were inspired by his new approach to the art of healing; laboratories had come into existence where new medicines were being prepared according to

Supplement

Rudolf Steiner's directions, and nursing homes were being opened where new ways of treatment were made available to patients. The people who asked Rudolf Steiner for the Curative Education Course had witnessed all this, and they had seen quite new possibilities blossom forth also in the various arts–painting, music, architecture, etc., in fact, they had come to know from their own experience that Anthroposophy was capable of inspiring every branch of life with new creative powers. And this knowledge gave them unlimited confidence in any advice received from Rudolf Steiner.

Besides all this, these people had just lived through the first World War. They had come to realise that times had changed, but they found that most people clung to the old ways of a kind of thinking which had been justified in earlier centuries, but which was not capable of running and controlling a world which had become so different. In fact, it was this antiquated kind of thinking which was itself responsible for the terrible situations confronting humanity. Old ideas were incapable of solving new problems, and it was obvious that worse situations would follow unless a sufficient number of human beings were prepared to awaken in their consciousness, and meet the demands of a changed world with new, creative ideas. We know now that there were not then enough human beings who had the courage to part with old and worn-out principles, and we have witnessed a second World War, far worse than the first. Many, many things that Rudolf Steiner predicted and gave warning of have since become shatteringly true. When we read his lectures of the years preceding, during and just after the first World War, we are struck by the clarity with which he foresaw the subsequent course of events, and we ask ourselves: Did he really say *all that,* publicly, to many, many people, as much as thirty and forty years ago? Did not anyone hear it? Were people unable to understand him? Did they not want to understand him when he did his utmost to make them realise, for the sake of their own welfare, the truth of the situation? Did no one take him seriously? We may well ask: Who is there who takes him seriously *today,* now that events have proved over and over again how right he was?

Those people who had found the impulse within their own hearts to devote their lives to the nursing and teaching of children in need of special care, they knew well that the same kind of thinking which had led to the first World War, would lead to another unless there were enough people with courage to change their outlook on life. They knew too that this kind of thinking was, in many cases, directly responsible even for the sick condition of these children. For many of these afflicted children are the victims of our modern civilisation.

A direct result of this wrong kind of thinking about man and the world, is the idea of Euthanasia. Recently this subject has once again stirred the minds of people; it has been discussed widely in the press and the general public has voiced opposing views on the matter. I do not want to be an alarmist, but we are gathered together here because we are interested in this question. We have the future destiny of these children at heart, we want to fight for their welfare. And just as it is wrong to be unnecessarily alarming, so it is wrong to bury one's head in the sand and avoid paying attention to important things that are happening.

We all know that the question of Euthanasia for seriously afflicted children has come up periodically many times before. It has then blown over, and it will blow over again. But one day we may have to face the issue seriously, and then everything will depend on *how* we can confront this problem. Shall we then be sufficiently equipped to stand the fight, to win the battle? It is up to us now to prepare ourselves in good time, before it is too late.

There were indeed many voices raised in favour of helping these children; but most of the arguments were not nearly strong enough. Just to quote an example, there was a woman who said: "As the mother of such a child I could never agree to Euthanasia." But there was another woman who held the opposite view; yet she too was the mother of such an afflicted child, but her wish was to end his suffering. Both views were born from love. This shows it is not enough to say: "As a mother I must say 'no'; as a priest I must say 'no'; as a medical doctor I must say 'no.'" For there are other people who are mothers and priests and medical officers too, and who, for the same reason, say "yes." When we follow all these controversies, we suddenly realise that all these arguments are born of personal opinions, and that opposing personal opinions may be born of the same motive. And we realise too that one day, if we should have to face the issue seriously, personal opinions will lead us nowhere. They will cut no ice at all. We can only hope to win this battle if, by then, we have managed to leave behind all personal opinions, to arrive at the objective truth of this problem. How can we find this objective truth, this unbiased point of view? Let us look at the origin of the idea of Euthanasia. How could such an idea arise at all?

When we look for the origin of the idea of Euthanasia, we find that it was born from that kind of thinking which, for some time now, has considered man to be but the highest animal; which for some time has believed that life arises from matter, that mind arises from matter. This school of thought firmly believes that, if only we progress sufficiently far in our knowledge of matter, we shall discover the secret of how, under certain complicated conditions, matter produces life, and of how matter produces spirit. To all people who share this view, matter is the primary given thing, and everything else has followed from it.

It is from this school of thought that the idea of Euthanasia has been born. Concerning the animal kingdom the phrase has been coined: The survival of the fittest. It has only been possible to consider applying this phrase to the kingdom of man because man was looked upon as being a descendant of the higher animals.

Now, if it is really true that we live in a world where things evolve quite by chance, where man has arisen somewhere and at some time, as the chance product of natural evolution; if it is true that, by some casual natural process, the transition has taken place from inorganic to organic matter, from unconscious existence to thinking consciousness; that the human mind arises from the matter of the brain and therefore also ceases to exist with the destruction of that same matter from which it has arisen; if all that is left of us after death is contained in the sum total of any valuable work which we may have done during our lifetime, and which has become part of the world, continuing to live on independent of its creator: if all this is true, then indeed we are led to look upon the life of a backward child as a useless and utterly wasted existence. But is all this really true? Is there a genuine foundation for all the assumptions on which such a judgement is based?

In view of the crushing evidence of the findings of modern science, man has come to doubt, and doubt very seriously, the existence of an immortal soul. And we shall find that it is just those scientists who are ruthlessly honest with themselves, who most strongly harbour this doubt, particularly when they find that, in their hearts, they wish it to be otherwise. They do not want to be guided in any way by personal wishes and preferences. In their judgement on these vital questions they want to be guided only by the objective results of their scientific research, and when they are confronted with the great riddles of the universe, they have come to admit that there are limits to human knowledge. Some philosophers and scientists even go so far as to declare that it is presumptuous for man to want to know certain great truths. They maintain that the ultimate questions on the evolution of the world, on human life on earth, on the existence of God, etc., will for ever remain impenetrable mysteries which we are not meant to solve nor even understand.

Rudolf Steiner, on the other hand, has made it very clear that the limits to human knowledge exist only so long as we ourselves do not strive to overcome these limits. Man's power of thinking enables him to sort out the bewildering multitude of sense impressions and, by bringing order into his observations, he is able to arrive at an ever greater understanding of himself and of the world around him. We know from experience that our thinking can be trained and developed. In studying mathematics, for example, we may not be able to grasp highly complicated formulae all at once, but we know that one day we shall be able to understand them, if we ourselves really want to grasp their meaning, and if we are ready to take all the necessary steps leading up to such an understanding. Whenever we ourselves make the effort to train and develop our thinking, we find that the limits to knowledge by which we were previously bound, recede further and further. It is exactly the same in physical space. Wherever we happen to be there are limits to our field of observation. We cannot look beyond a certain horizon. But as soon as we ourselves begin to walk towards that horizon, things and places enter our field of experience which previously were beyond it. The further we go, the more we see and learn about the world in which we live, and thus our life experience continues to grow. It is true, of course, when we walk through space, that things disappear from view behind us at the same rate at which they appear in front. Nevertheless, they are not lost to us because we can retain them in our memory. Rudolf Steiner himself had an unshakeable trust in the power of thinking. He has shown us, step by step, the path which he has himself taken in his study of thinking – a path on which we can follow him if we wish to see for ourselves – and he has spoken in detail of the results of his investigations. And these results can be understood with ordinary, logical thinking, even if we are not ready to follow in his footsteps and train our own thinking and observation in the way he has shown that they can be trained and developed.

Rudolf Steiner has proved that life is not produced by matter but that, on the contrary, matter is a residue of life processes. In the same way, it is not the brain which produces the thinking, for thinking as a living spiritual capacity existed in the universe long before there was

Supplement

any material brain. In fact, it was the living thinking which created the brain as an instrument through which it was enabled to manifest itself within a world of matter.

I would like to use a very simple picture to illustrate what I mean. Let us imagine a violinist who takes up his violin and plays the most beautiful music. Then he puts the violin in its case again and walks away. Now let us assume that this has been observed by another man, a man who has never before seen a violin or met a violinist. This man also takes the violin and himself tries to produce the same kind of music which he has heard from the instrument a few moments before. He has watched carefully and thinks he has seen exactly how it was done. To his utter surprise no wonderful music arises from the violin however, but only horrible noises emerge. This man says to himself: "I know that there is music inside this violin, for I myself have heard it come from the instrument with my own ears. I will investigate the matter. I will take the violin to pieces and examine carefully the material of which it is made. I know that, in this way, I must discover the music sooner or later. I know that music is hidden, or at least produced inside the violin, because I have heard it coming out, and if only I progress sufficiently in my exact knowledge of the material structure of the violin, I am bound to find the music.

Now in the case of the violin, we would all say: But, how foolish of the man to try and argue things in that way! We all know that the music is not hidden inside a violin. The music lives in the musician and he merely uses the violin as an instrument through which he can make apparent and perceptible to other people the melody that lives in him. Nature did not simply produce a violin which poured forth music. We know that, first of all, man himself existed, and there was music living within him. And because there was music in him, he began to sing, and he created for himself also instruments through which he could make this music perceptible.

In regard to the violin we say: How foolish to see things in that way! Yet in regard to the human brain, we adopt that same foolish attitude without ever questioning it. Just as the music arises from the violin, only when there is a capable violinist to produce it, so the thoughts arise in the brain, only when a capable thinker is dwelling within to produce them. The brain of a corpse does not produce thoughts, for the man who lived in the body has left it and has taken with him his living capacity of thinking. When a man lies in a deep dreamless sleep, his brain is not producing thoughts because, during sleep, he withdraws with his thinking consciousness from his body. We shall never arrive at music by examining the wood of which a violin is made, but we can approach the musician and learn from him the secret of his music. Similarly, we shall never solve the riddle of thinking by examining the matter of the brain, but we must ask of man himself the secret of his thinking; and here each man is nearest to himself. I may not be able to know all at once how another person thinks, but if only I take the trouble, I can observe myself and I can find out how I myself set about it when I wish to gain clarity on some problem, by thinking it through. I shall soon discover that I am not compelled to think any thoughts which my brain wants me to think. This may be the case sometimes, when I simply allow my thoughts to drift along idly from one subject to another, from one fragment of memory to another. But it does not happen when I myself decide on the course of my thinking, when I succeed in thinking through to the end a certain line of thought which I myself have decided to pursue. Then I find that I am free to lead my thoughts in any direction, and that I can fill them with a content of my own choosing. I know quite well then that it is not my brain which is doing all this on its own, compelled by chemical and physiological processes within its cells: I know then that I myself am thinking, and that I am merely making use of my brain as an instrument.

In his book The Philosophy of Spiritual Activity Rudolf Steiner has shown very clearly how we can arrive at an understanding of the true nature of thinking Man is indeed more than the mere sum of the material processes in his body; man cannot be explained from the matter of his body. When we stand before the corpse of a beloved friend we know that all we have loved and treasured in the living person has vanished from the body and the body is like an empty house. We begin to realise then that we human beings are really "invisible" people; that is to say all our qualities such as thinking, feeling and willing, love and hatred, joy and sorrow, are invisible and, on earth, only betray their presence by finding expression in matter. The sorrow of a person may find expression in his features; the sorrow itself is invisible. The love of one person for another may find expression in words and deeds; the love itself is invisible.

Now just as there are essential qualities in man which are invisible, so there are essential qualities in the world around us which are themselves invisible, yet which betray their presence by their visible deeds and achievements in the material processes of the world. We

Supplement

know quite well from experience in our own man-made world that nothing comes into being just by itself, without someone doing it. When we need a house to live in, someone must build it; when we need clothes to wear, someone must sew them; when we need meals to eat, someone must prepare them. We know that none of these things will happen by themselves. And yet, when we look out into nature and see the unfolding of the seasons, the ripening of the fruit, the wonderful movements of the starry bodies in the universe, we so easily take it for granted that all these miracles happen somehow by themselves. We know that we have to work very hard indeed to learn geometry; and we should have to take great pains to draw accurately before we could produce spirals of the kind which appear in every little daisy flower. We know that an architect has to master a tremendous amount of knowledge before he can build a bridge which will securely carry heavy traffic. But now let us look at the miraculous construction of the human skeleton. Surely, we must stand in wonder and admiration before the construction of a thigh bone which is capable of supporting very great weight with the least possible amount of material. Wherever we look in the world around us, we find that everything has been built with wisdom. And there must be a very wise guidance which maintains this complicated universe and keeps it going.

Wherever we look at the world, and however we examine it, we find no confirmation of the assumption that spirit could ever be born from matter, but we find plenty of evidence of its being the other way about: there was living spirit before matter was ever created. The world of matter was born from the world of spirit. And it is the spirit in man which can find the way to the spirit in Nature; it is the invisible qualities in man which can build the bridge to the invisible forces of the world.

If the soul and spirit of man are not born from the matter of his body, through some highly complicated chemical processes, if, on the contrary, the body of matter owes its creation to the deeds of soul and spirit, then the soul and spirit of man must be able to exist independently of a material body. The soul and spirit of man must have existed before they came to take up an abode in a body of flesh and blood, and they will live on after this body has been discarded at the moment of death. Man is immortal in his soul and spirit, and the world of matter is but a passing phase in evolution.

In many books and lectures Rudolf Steiner has developed this line of thought, and with the utmost clarity has shown that the immortal soul and spirit of man do not dwell once only in a physical body on earth, but they incarnate, again and again, into every civilisation, into every epoch of history, throughout the whole of earthly evolution.

The idea of reincarnation as such is by no means new. It can indeed be found in many religions and in many philosophies. Nevertheless, it is entirely new in the form in which Rudolf Steiner has presented it, a form which is true to the needs of mankind in this twentieth century. It has been much more widely known in olden times, and it has had to be forgotten in order to be regained in quite a new way. We may ask: How is it possible that such vital knowledge could have been forgotten so completely? When we study history we discover that men in olden times knew a great many things which have been completely forgotten in modern times, but they then knew them from divine revelation, and they had to lose this God-given wisdom and knowledge, in order to make it truly their own by re-conquering it of their own free will, by their own effort, through their own free deeds of recognition.

I will just mention one outstanding example of such a disappearance of well-established knowledge in history. America was well-known in ancient times. We have ample proof of the fact that the inhabitants of Europe and of other continents, had knowledge of and contact with America; and yet the existence of America was forgotten so completely, that it was possible to re-discover it in the fifteenth century as something entirely new and hitherto unknown. We may well ask: How was it possible to forget the existence of a vast continent? And yet we see that it did happen.

In a similar way, the knowledge of reincarnation has had to be forgotten, in order to be re-discovered through the new powers of human consciousness, which have meanwhile been developing through the successive epochs of history.

I have repeatedly heard people say: "Why did I have to be born in this dreadful century? I wish I had lived at the time of the old Greek culture, or at the time of the Renaissance," etc. I have also heard people say: "I am terribly glad that I have been born into just this century. I would not have missed this epoch for anything, and I am very relieved that I did not have to come into the darkness of the Middle Ages." Then again I have heard it said: "Why should one person be born in the slums, to live in poverty and squalor, inheriting a sick body, and with no chance of a good education or a good life before him, while another person is born into a well-to-do home, into cultured surroundings, inheriting a healthy body, receiving a good education as a foundation for a brilliant career? Apart from the situations in which the misfortunes of a person are obviously due to his own faults and misdeeds, there seems to be a great deal of injustice in the world, and some people have to bear immense suffering for no apparent reason and through no apparent fault of their own, whereas other people are extremely lucky, again for no apparent reason and through no apparent merit on their part."

Life is indeed full of things which do not make sense, until one begins to see them in the light of reincarnation; and then they fall into place. When we think things through to their ultimate consequence, we arrive at the idea of reincarnation, both as a logical conclusion and as a matter of experience. The fact that we may meet a number of people who battle against this idea, is no proof of its being wrong, for we know from history, for instance, that the early Christians had to sacrifice their lives for a belief which today is firmly established in many parts of the world; and the forerunners of modern science were burnt at the stake even as late as three and four hundred years ago for daring to proclaim truths which today are taught to every schoolboy.

Against the background of such thoughts, the life of a backward child begins to look very different. It is not then a wasted life, an injustice of destiny, nor is it the only chance that is offered to him. If it were the only chance, then the outlook would indeed be, in many cases, entirely hopeless. But if it is seen as one life in a long chain of incarnations, we gain an entirely new perspective and, in proportion, it will appear but as one bad day out of a series of good days. We do not like bad days, we do not like pain and suffering. We like happy days, we like joys and pleasures, love and success. But we do know that we could not live on pleasures alone. When we look back on our own lives, we know quite well that we have learnt far more from the painful experiences of life than from all our pleasures. A life of everlasting pleasure would make us easy-going, superficial and irresponsible. It is invariably the hard lessons which teach us the wisdom of life. There is indeed sense in suffering, and though we do not wish anyone to suffer, we yet cannot deny that valuable treasures have been born from it. I know a doctor in a small town which I have often visited. He was always very much loved by his patients, and they had great confidence in him. But one day I learnt that he himself had been seriously ill and had very nearly died. And people were saying that since his illness, he was a much better doctor even than he had been before. He had always been a good doctor because he tried to feel with his patients and imagine what it must be like to be suffering pain. After his illness, however, he no longer had to imagine what it must be like to be very ill: he knew from his own experience.

To give another example: I met a lady some time ago who is the mother of several children. There was one backward child among them, and she said of this child, "He was much more difficult than all the other children put together. I had a very hard time with him. But, through his very difficulties, he opened my eyes to so many things in life of which I had been completely ignorant, that I am immensely grateful to him. I owe more to him and I have learnt more from him than I have learnt from any of the other children."

I repeat that we do not, of course, wish anyone to suffer, nor do we like suffering the better for having recognised the value of experiences which can be gained from it. Yet such a recognition does enable us to meet it in a different frame of mind when it happens to come our way. Such a thought can indeed become a well of strength and courage in any difficult situation. It will not permit us to slide into a mood of hopelessness. We shall no longer crumble under the apparent senselessness or injustice of life, but we shall learn to look upon suffering as we would look upon a probation to which we submit voluntarily, in order to prove our ability to endure it. Obstacles will not then prevent our progress, but they will challenge us to grow strong against them and to overcome them. And our question will then be: "What is the positive aspect of this difficulty which comes to meet me? What does it want to teach me? Dreadful though this blow seems to be, just what does it want to tell me that I have never learnt before?" If only we can achieve such an attitude towards the troubles of life, we shall have won half the battle. We will not then blame destiny, or the world situation, or other people, for what befalls us, but courageously place the responsibility for our life upon our own shoulders, where it belongs.

Now-a-days, every single person should begin to feel responsible for world affairs. We ourselves make history. We ourselves create the conditions for our own lives. If we remain as we are, conditions will become worse, because to stand still means to regress. The world will only change when we change.

Serious study, for instance, will change a man. Real study will collect our forces and strengthen us, and we ourselves are different after we have made the effort to think big thoughts, after we have filled our minds with great and noble ideas and have lived with them for a while. And once our attitude has changed, our deeds too will change; and thereby the world will become different. Our thoughts can become creative deeds, and it matters greatly whether or no a backward child is surrounded by people who try to be creatively active in their thinking. It enhances his possibility of recovery or at least of improvement. It matters just what we think when we work and live with these children. It makes all the difference whether we just soothe a child and have pity on him, helping him to while away the awful span of such a limited existence in as pleasant a way as possible, or whether we inwardly say to him: Why have you chosen such difficulties, and what have you come to learn from such a life? Who are you to have taken up such a burden to carry?

Just in regard to afflicted children it is worth our while to picture in detail, and quite consequently, what it means if the soul dies with the death of the body, or again if the soul is immortal and sent down to life on earth for a purpose. If man were but the highest animal and his soul and spirit vanish with his body, then perhaps, after all Euthanasia might be justified. If, on the other hand, man has an immortal soul and spirit, an eternal individuality, then he is indeed worth fighting for, even when he appears in the guise of a backward child, and the practise of Euthanasia would be a serious and even criminal interference with his destiny. He would then be prevented from learning the lessons, receiving the corrections and gaining the experiences which he needs and which he has set himself to find in living the life of a backward child.

People who believe thoughts to be but secretions of the brain have no confidence in the creative power of thinking. They often say: "But what difference does it make to the world what I think? The world takes no notice of my thinking, and I cannot hope to be able to steer the course of events in a different direction. If Euthanasia should one day be introduced against my wishes, what can I do about it?" But here is the point where we must realise that we can do something about it. For it will not be possible to enforce Euthanasia for afflicted children if there is a sufficient body of people who oppose it and, what is more, who know exactly why they do so. They will not then voice personal opinions, born of instinctive feelings, but they will pronounce their judgement on the strength of the objective truth which is found in the realm of clear thinking. It is for the sake of our children that we must begin to think anew. We must grasp the fact that thoughts are not mere shadowy reflections of physical "realities," but these "realities" owe their existence to the power of thinking, and they can be altered and remodelled through new creative ideas. When ignorant children play with fire, they are unconscious of the danger. When ignorant adults begin to play with the idea of Euthanasia, nobody knows where it will end.

Reflections such as these enable us to see the difficulties of an afflicted child in quite a new light. The eternal individuality of man needs a material body for his life on earth. This body is his earthly house wherein he dwells. It is at the same time his instrument, through which he can perceive the world and work in the world. Now we may be faced with two possibilities: the individuality of an afflicted child may have great capacities, but only a sick body, a damaged instrument, at his disposal. On the other hand, a child may lack ability, and therefore be unable to make use of the most perfect organs. A great pianist would not dream of giving a concert on an old upright piano which is broken and badly out of tune. With all his outstanding ability, he could not possibly give a decent performance. On the other hand, a man utterly lacking in musical ability could not give a decent performance either, even though he had the most perfect grand piano at his disposal. Thus children sometimes have great gifts, but the organs are destroyed or damaged through which these gifts could find expression. Or children may inhabit perfect, healthy bodies, but are unable to develop the ability to use them as instruments. Our methods of treatment will then have to be varied accordingly.

Similar external symptoms may indeed be caused by quite different inner dispositions, and Rudolf Steiner has pointed out in the Curative Education Course that we merely waste our time in attempting to cure superficial symptoms. We can only really help the child when we try to penetrate through the symptoms to the very substance of the illness. The study of retarded children is indeed a long and slow study, but ultimately it leads us very far in our knowledge of man.

These children are calling to awaken us to the greater realities of life, to revise our ideas of man and the universe, because we cannot solve the riddle of their existence with our ordinary conventional way of thinking. This conventional way of thinking concerns itself with all the facts of our waking life; but it does not penetrate into the hours of sleep which constitute one-third of our life time. Our memory embraces only that portion of our life which is spent in waking consciousness. The part which belongs to sleep is wrapped in mystery, its content withheld from our knowledge; and yet it belongs to us and we know that it conceals some of the most important factors necessary for our daily existence. For deeply hidden behind the darkness of sleep there lies the well of life which renews us every night. That is why we feel dissatisfied with any world conception, any philosophy, which fails to reach the deeper realities of life; these exceptional children make us go in search of these deeper realities, go in search of the whole truth, for we can only begin to understand them when we arrive at a concept of man which embraces every aspect of his existence. In their present condition these children are severely handicapped, often in a way which cannot easily be remedied. They are bound by this condition which is a heritage from the past, and it is often impossible to cure it completely within the span of one life-time. Yet we can always begin today to plant new seeds for the future. We are slaves of the past, but we are masters of the future. And past and future meet in the present. In their present state of illness these children are indeed slaves of the past, but this very state of illness contains at the same time the seeds of freedom for the future, and we are called upon to help them to master the future.

Address List

The Independent Rudolf Steiner Schools and homes for those in need of Special Care.

Bridge House,
Padworth, Reading,
Berkshire RG7 4JU
Tel: 01734 713176
Home for young people and adults aged from 16.

Bryn Garth,
Much Birch,
Hereford HR2 8HJ
Tel: 01981 540284
Residential community for young men.

Cotswold Chine House School,
Box, Nr. Stroud,
Glos. GL6 0AG
Tel: 01453 83 2398
A residential co-educational school for emotionally disturbed children aged 10-16.

Garvald Centre,
2, Montpelier Terrace,
Edinburgh EH10 4NF
Tel: 01312 28 3712
Day & residential centre for training young people.

Garvald Community Enterprises,
The Engine Shed,
19, St. Leonard's
Edinburgh EH8 9SD
Tel: 01316 22 00040
Provides training at an employment level & work experience for people with and without special needs.

Garvald Home Farm,
Dolphinton, West Linton,
Borders EH46 7HJ
Tel: 01968 82238
Bio-Dynamic farm home/work for adults.

Garvald West Linton,
West Linton,
Borders, EH46 7HJ
Tel: 01968 82211
Residential training centre for young people aged 16 upwards.

Nutley Hall,
Nutley, Uckfield,
East Sussex TN22 3NJ
Tel: 01825 712696
Residential Home for adults over age 18.

Peredur Trust,
Trebullom, Altarnun,
Launceston,
Cornwall PL15 7RF
Tel: 01566 86575
Here are two residential centres for young men one craft/garden oriented one a farm.

Philpots Manor School & Further Training Centre
West Hoathly,
East Grinstead,
Sussex RH19 4PR
Tel: 01342 810268
A co-educational boarding school for children with emotional and behavioural disturbances, aged 6-16

Potterspury Lodge School,
Towcester
Northants, NN12 7LL
Tel: 01908 542912
For emotionally disturbed children of average intelligence, having severe learning/social/personality problems.

Solden Hill House,
Banbury Road,
Byfield,
Daventry,
Northants. NN11 6UA
Tel: 01327 260234
Residential home for mentally handicapped adults.

Sunfield Childrens Homes,
Clent,
Stourbridge,
West Midlands DY9 9PB
Tel: 01562 882253
Residential school for girls & boys aged 6-19

St. Christopher's School,
Carisbrooke Lodge,
Westbury Park,
Bristol BS6 7JE
Tel: 0117 9736875/9733301
Day & boarding school for boys & girls 7-19

The Association of Camphill Communities
Secretary's Office,
Gawain House,
56, Welham Road,
North Malton,
North Yorks. YO17 9DP
Tel: (01653) 694197
There are many different Camphill Homes/Schools/Communities covering all age groups throughout the UK, contact the secretary for details.

For worldwide addresses please contact **Committee for Steiner Special Education c/o Philpots Manor School** at above address and **Association of Camphill Communities.**

Bibliography:

Books on education by:
Rudolf Steiner *(not necessarily in print)*

The Education of the Child
Essentials of Education
Roots of Education
The Kingdom of Childhood
Practical Course for Teachers
Education and Modem Spiritual Life
Discussions with Teachers
The Spiritual Ground of Education
Curative Education

By other authors *(not necessarily in print)*

"*The Recovery of Man in Childhood*" by A. C. Harwood
"*Rudolf Steiner Education*" by L. F. Edmunds
"*The Wisdom in Fairy Tales*" by Ursula Grahl
"*The Way of a Child*" by A. C. Harwood
"*Childhood*" by C. von Heydebrand
"*Children in Need of Special Care*" by Thomas J. Weiss - Souvenir Press, London ISBN 0 285 64850 0
"*Therapy in Music for Handicapped Children*" by Paul Nordoff & Clive Robbins - Victor Gollancz
"*Play Therapy - A creative approach to play therapy for the mentally handicapped child.*" by Ursula Bartning. Gavemer Publishing, Sydney. ISBN 0 947343 07 5
"*The Food We Eat, herbs and nutrition*" by Maria Geuter. Anastasi Ltd. UK. ISBN 0-9524403-3-4 (Contains a chapter on the Four Temperaments and the feeding of small children).